TEACHING READERS IN
POST-TRUTH AMERICA

TEACHING READERS IN POST-TRUTH AMERICA

ELLEN C. CARILLO

UTAH STATE UNIVERSITY PRESS
Logan

© 2018 by University Press of Colorado

Published by Utah State University Press
An imprint of University Press of Colorado
245 Century Circle, Suite 202
Louisville, Colorado 80027

 The University Press of Colorado is a proud member of the Association of University Presses.

The University Press of Colorado is a cooperative publishing enterprise supported, in part, by Adams State University, Colorado State University, Fort Lewis College, Metropolitan State University of Denver, Regis University, University of Colorado, University of Northern Colorado, Utah State University, and Western State Colorado University.

∞ This paper meets the requirements of the ANSI/NISO Z39.48-1992 (Permanence of Paper).

ISBN: 978-1-60732-790-5 (pbk.)
ISBN: 978-1-60732-791-2 (ebook)
DOI: https://doi.org/10.7330/9781607327912

Library of Congress Cataloging-in-Publication Data

Names: Carillo, Ellen C., author.
Title: Teaching readers in post-truth America / Ellen C. Carillo.
Description: Logan : Utah State University Press, [2018] | Includes bibliographical references and index.
Identifiers: LCCN 2018000466| ISBN 9781607327905 (pbk.) | ISBN 9781607327912 (ebook)
Subjects: LCSH: Reading (Higher education)—United States. | Rhetoric—Political aspects—United States. | Evidence. | Reading comprehension—United States. | Critical thinking—United States.
Classification: LCC LB2395.3 .C35 2018 | DDC 418/.40711—dc23
LC record available at https://lccn.loc.gov/2018000466

Funding for the indexing of this book came from the University of Connecticut's Scholarship Facilitation Fund.

Back cover art: Joseph A. Gerber

CONTENTS

TEACHING READERS IN
POST-TRUTH AMERICA

1
INTRODUCTION

After Donald J. Trump was elected the forty-fifth president of the United States in November 2016, I felt what many others felt: shock, anger, disappointment, even fear. Then, another emotion kicked in: guilt. As an English instructor and specifically a writing instructor for more than fifteen years and a writing program coordinator for ten years, I felt partially responsible for the outcome of the election. Had I not been teaching my students to reject the kind of rhetoric that Trump employed? Had I failed at teaching them the importance of evidence to making an argument, the significance of both citing sources and the credibility of those sources? Had I neglected to teach them the value of precision in expression and the importance of context to constructing meaning? Had we not addressed what it means to be ethical readers, writers, and communicators who undertake this work in responsible ways? Almost half the country voted for Trump. How many of these voters had I taught?

Those who voted for Trump, some of whom may be reading this book, could not even celebrate or enjoy their victory. Whether they felt silenced by their Democratic colleagues or resentful of how the media portrayed the election results as thoroughly shocking, these voters were also angry, distracted, and disheartened. Despite feeling some of the same emotions, people across the country had seemingly become even more divided.[1] It is the combination of this political divisiveness and the increase in the use of post-truth rhetoric that brought about this book. No matter where readers fall on the left-right political divide, though, I think *Teaching Readers in Post-Truth America* explores something on which we can all agree: we have found ourselves at a pivotal moment in which the stakes of literacy

DOI: 10.7330/9781607327912.c001

education are pretty high. Certainly, we have been privy to any number of previous "literacy crises," as well as political crises wherein high-ranking political figures, including presidents, have been exposed as dishonest. We have also witnessed the circulation of "fake news" in the form of rumors, hoaxes, and salacious news stories.[2] What we have not witnessed before, though, are the cultural and ideological shifts that characterize our present moment. In an article by the BBC's Sean Coughlin, philosopher A. C. Grayling describes our contemporary moment through the concept of post-truth:[3] "The whole post-truth phenomenon is about, 'My opinion is worth more than the facts.' It's about how I feel about things. It's terribly narcissistic. It's been empowered by the fact that you can publish your opinion. You used to need a pot of paint and a balaclava to publish your opinion, if you couldn't get a publisher. But all you need now is an iPhone. Everyone can publish their opinion—and if you disagree with me, it's an attack on me and not my ideas."

As Grayling points out, post-truth culture thrives particularly in a society that values opinions more than facts and, moreover, has as many outlets for people to share those opinions as there are outlets to disseminate facts. Still, the iPhone is certainly not the root of our post-truth culture. These roots have been traced—for different ends—to any number of sources. Some see the roots of our post-truth culture in Evangelical and other religious sects that preach against accepting a secular worldview over a religious (i.e., a Christian) worldview wherein the latter is characterized by a "deep distrust of the media" and "scientific consensus" (Worthen 2017). Others see our post-truth culture as an outgrowth of the postmodern rejection of an objective reality (D'Ancona 2017; Cadwalladr 2017), while many maintain that post-truth rhetoric is not only as old as political rhetoric but that they are one and the same.

Despite the current climate, in his dual biography of George Orwell and Winston Churchill, Thomas E. Ricks (2017:269–70) comments on the central role objective truth has historically played: "The struggle to see things as they are is perhaps the fundamental driver of Western civilization. There is a long but direct line from Aristotle and Archimedes to Locke, Hume, Mill and Darwin, and from there through Orwell and Churchill to Martin Luther King writing his 'Letter from Birmingham City Jail.' It is the agreement that objective reality exists, that people of goodwill can perceive it, and that other people will change their views when presented with the facts of the matter." A post-truth culture in which there is no agreement that objective reality exists puts educators in a seemingly untenable position. If no one agrees on what constitutes accuracy or facts, then where does this leave us?

As its title and introduction thus far suggest, this book takes the position that we are, in fact, living in a post-truth culture. The *Oxford English Dictionary* defines "post-truth" as "relating to or denoting circumstances in which objective facts are less influential in shaping public opinion than appeals to emotion and personal belief." While the media and other sources have outlined the ways the Trump administration has perpetuated this culture,[4] it is important to remember—alongside Grayling, as well as those who posit other origins—that our post-truth culture has evolved over time and is the result of far more than the election of a single president.

While origin stories can be very interesting, this book is more concerned with the implications of this post-truth culture, particularly for education. Philosopher Michael P. Lynch (2016:63) begins to parse these implications: "When you can't agree on your principles of evidence and rationality, you can't agree on the facts. And, if you can't agree on the facts, you can hardly agree on what to do in the face of the facts, and that just increases tribalization, and so on and on in a recurring loop." In a culture that does not agree on the principles of evidence and rationality or on facts, how does one teach reading, writing, and thinking?

John Duffy (2017:18) lays out some options for instructors: "We can accept the language and culture of post-truth as the new normal in which facts are not facts, assertions need not be burdened by evidence, and truth is what the powerful say it is. Or," he continues, "we can choose to speak, write, and teach in a language that resists the culture of post-truth . . . a language of argument grounded in such virtues as honesty, accountability, generosity, courage, and radical humility."

Bruce McComiskey (2017:38) argues that our field is uniquely positioned to respond: "The fact is, rhetoric and composition has had the tools to combat post-truth rhetoric for years, and we, as a community of scholars and teachers, need to double-down on those tools." Moreover, writes McComiskey (2017:43), "A plan for action already exists in disciplinary white papers like the *Framework for Success in Postsecondary Writing* and the *WPA Outcomes Statement for First-Year Composition*," which promote values including curiosity, openness, engagement, creativity, persistence, responsibility, flexibility, meta-cognition, critical thinking, analysis, and rhetorical knowledge.

Although not directly addressing post-truth culture, this concept nonetheless seems to inflect Linda Adler-Kassner's March 2017 Conference on College Composition and Communication (CCCC) presidential address, wherein she details our field's commitment to preparing students to "question assumptions they've made, to shake up what might have been inert, to adapt or change prior knowledge." She continues, "Learning involves being comfortable with the discomfort that this invokes, because this discomfort is critical for changing one's mind— and real learning happens when that change occurs, when learners develop new or deeper ways of thinking and doing. Writing plays a critical role here. When we work with students to study writing, we are helping them look at how expectations for writing or products of writing reflect deeper commitments and epistemologies, at how what is written tells us about how people work with and from expectations" (Adler-Kassner 2017).

As insightful and promising as these accounts are, they neglect to think about what a post-truth culture means for readers. How does it affect reading? How does it affect readers? How might it affect the way we teach reading? For example, are there reading practices that are "grounded in such virtues as honesty, accountability, generosity, courage, and radical humility" that would complement the argumentative writing practices Duffy describes? I also wonder how reading practices, like the writing practices Adler-Kassner details, might "reflect deeper commitments and epistemologies."

Although these scholars don't address reading, I think they would agree—and I think we all would agree, no matter our political leanings—that readers generally, and our students specifically, are under unprecedented pressure within this post-truth culture to navigate the range of texts (broadly defined) that vie for attention and acceptance. Conceiving of reading as a practice of constructing meaning, this book argues that foregrounding and teaching the interpretive practice of reading alongside writing in the academy is one way of responding to this contemporary moment and is absolutely crucial to preparing our students to participate in an information-rich democratic society.

This book explores the importance of teaching in postsecondary institutions and in first-year writing courses, specifically, what is most often called "critical reading."[5] In particular, this book addresses the stakes associated with doing so in a post-truth culture. This work is especially important because we know from large-scale studies (the Citation Project, National Assessment of Educational Progress 2016, Project SAILS 2017) and students' scores on the SAT Verbal/Critical Reading Portion and the ACT Reading Portion that their critical reading abilities, including their most basic comprehension skills, are rather weak. Moreover, studies also indicate that these digital natives are largely incapable of reading to discern the credibility of online sources and are "easily duped" (Stanford History Education Group 2016). If we (optimistically) believe that the value of credibility and the existence of objective reality (among other foundational beliefs crucial to a fully functioning democracy) are not entirely (or forever) lost, this book considers the specific reading-centered interventions the field of rhetoric and composition can make, as well as what we might draw on from other fields to further enrich our contributions.

Teaching Readers in Post-Truth America builds on my earlier work wherein I argue for teaching within the expansive, reflective, and meta-cognitive framework of mindful reading. More than ever it seems that students not only need direct instruction in reading but that to position students to transfer what they learn about reading across courses and contexts, instructors need to teach reading within expansive contexts like the mindful reading framework I detail in *Securing a Place for Reading In Composition: The Importance of Teaching for Transfer* (Carillo 2015) and elsewhere. Although we have seen a revival of attention to reading within the field of rhetoric and composition, reading still remains under-theorized, making it that much more important to take the time to explore how it fits into the field's larger response[6] and resistance to this post-truth culture.

CHAPTERS

Chapter 2 considers the similarities between the Common Core State Standards' (CCSS) English Language Arts Standards and the reading pedagogy of the New Critics. Specifically, this chapter explores the stakes associated with severing the relationship between readers and texts within a post-truth culture, as well as cultivating in students a reverence for texts. Examining largely unknown revisions of the New Criticism's reading pedagogy, the chapter contends that these revisions should serve as a model of how the Common Core State Standards might be revised to reconnect readers to the process of reading and to better and more accurately represent how meaning is composed through reading.

Building on chapter 2's discussion of the CCSS, chapter 3 contends that no matter how consistently the standards try to push affect and emotion aside to privilege objectivity, research continues to indicate that learning is both a rational and an emotional process. The standards' devaluing of emotion is a worrisome prospect in a climate where it would seemingly be especially productive to help students cultivate an awareness and understanding of how emotions inform beliefs. As such, chapter 3 explores how situating emotion—specifically empathy—as a way of composing meaning and constructing knowledge complements more rationally driven modes of reading in the classroom. In addition to making emotions and empathy in particular more central to our teaching practices, this chapter also argues for considering how emotion functions in our research, particularly participant-based research. By pointing to an unexamined tradition of "empathic research" within the field of rhetoric and composition, this chapter argues for continuing that tradition by considering more holistic methods of "reading" data.

Taking its cue from Frank Farmer and Phillip Arrington's pronouncement that "imitation might be seriously rethought," chapter 4 explores the opportunities that open up for literacy instruction when we think beyond imitative writing practices and consider what it might mean to model sound reading practices for our students. This chapter focuses on the practice of annotation as a way to directly teach reading in the classroom. Because annotation concretizes the invisible act of reading, it can be used to model the work "expert" readers do. Although the demise of formalist methods of teaching writing also meant the rejection of imitative and modeling exercises, this chapter maintains that imitative exercises are prevalent in classrooms—despite the lack of scholarship that might suggest otherwise—and that bringing them to light is an important step to theorizing and supporting this pedagogy. Ultimately, chapter 4 considers how instructors might explore with students the largely unappreciated dialogic, dynamic, and transformative potential of imitation and modeling activities. Such activities provide opportunities for students to study and imitate expert reading practices that are characterized by flexibility and openness, reading practices that in a Freireian sense are crucial to reading the word and the world.

Chapter 5 provides an overview of the previous chapters to highlight the key concepts and ideas therein. Although the chapter does not deny the importance of the resources and pedagogical approaches explored in these earlier chapters, it details how some of rhetoric and composition's foundational values and principles may complicate the field's response to the current climate. Specifically, this chapter addresses how the field's prioritizing of logos over pathos, its over-reliance on the teaching of the simplistic argumentative essay, and its lack of attention to psychological research pose unique challenges as rhetoric and composition articulates and mobilizes its response to the current post-truth culture. Chapter 5 contends that anticipating and understanding the obstacles that may lie ahead is crucial to strengthening that response.

2
THEORETICAL FIRST PRINCIPLES

I first heard of the Common Core State Standards (CCSS), developed by the National Governors Association Center for Best Practices and the Council of Chief State School Officers, from one of my colleagues in rhetoric and composition.[7] Released in 2010 and adopted by all but a few states, the CCSS outline literacy standards (among other standards, including those for mathematical education) for reading and writing in K–12 English Language Arts, as well as across other disciplines. The CCSS provide a "vision of what it means to be a literate person who is prepared for success in the 21st century" and aim to foster "success in college, career, and life" (National Governors Association Center for Best Practices and Council of Chief State School Officers 2010). What I heard about the standards sounded promising: a curriculum that focused not just on literature but on what were being called "informational texts" and the promise—at least my colleague assured me—that students would therefore enter college more prepared to read the expository and nonfiction prose we often expected them to read in first-year writing courses and beyond.

But as I looked more closely at the CCSS, I realized that I had seen them before—or something an awful lot like them—in the reading pedagogy of the New Critics. As this chapter explores, these national standards depend on a reductive understanding of reading that seems to benefit the standards' stakeholders more than American students. Because this kind of reading is especially dangerous in our current post-truth culture, this chapter describes ways secondary-level instructors can work against the CCSS in their classrooms to better prepare students

DOI: 10.7330/9781607327912.c002

not only for college-level reading but for participating in an information-rich democracy.

In bringing issues associated with the CCSS and seemingly only related to secondary-level literacy instruction to the attention of postsecondary literacy instructors (i.e., the likely audience for this book), this chapter contributes to recent efforts to move beyond the boundaries that usually separate those teaching at different levels of the curriculum. Following the lead of the newly formed Modern Language Association's K–16 Alliances, as well as edited collections such as *What Is College-Level Writing?* volumes 1 and 2 (Sullivan and Tinberg 2006; Sullivan, Tinberg, and Blau 2010), *What Is College Reading?* (Horning, Gollnitz, and Haller 2017), and *Deep Reading: Teaching Reading in the Writing Classroom* (Sullivan, Tinberg, and Blau 2017), all of which put essays written by secondary and postsecondary instructors in dialogue with each other, this chapter contends that such dialogue allows us to see literacy education as happening on a continuum and that doing so is not only productive but necessary. The more opportunities secondary and postsecondary instructors have to engage each other and talk about their approaches, expectations, and the constraints within which they teach, the more informed the pedagogies at both levels will be.

TRACING THE SIMILARITIES BETWEEN THE NEW CRITICAL READING PEDAGOGY AND THE CCSS

Cleanth Brooks and Robert Penn Warren's directive to pay attention to "the object in itself" in their 1938 textbook *Understanding Poetry* has seemingly evolved into the theoretical model for reading outlined in the *Revised Publisher's Criteria for the Common Core State Standards*, the document intended for curricula developers and publishers who support the implementation of the Common Core. That document insists that the center of literacy instruction must be the "text itself," and "everything included in the surrounding materials should be thoughtfully considered and justified before being included . . . surrounding materials should be included only when necessary so as not to distract from the text itself" (Coleman and Pimentel 2012:10). Almost seventy-five years before the first version of the "Publisher's Criteria," Brooks and Warren took literature instructors to task in their "Letter to the Teacher," the preface to *Understanding Poetry*, for the state of early twentieth-century literary instruction. They described the "overpowering temptation" on the part of teachers to find "a substitute for the poem as the object of study." They explain, "The substitutes are various, but the most common ones are: 1. Paraphrase of logical and narrative content; 2. Study of biographical and historical materials; 3. Inspirational and didactic interpretation" (Brooks and Warren 1938:xi). As is well-known, Brooks, Warren, and other New Critics strongly rejected the use of biographical and historical information in literary study—what the "Publisher's Criteria" seemingly calls "supporting materials"—and maintained that the poem must be treated "as an object in itself," just as the Common Core regularly describes the importance of grasping fully the "text itself."

The similarities between these two reading pedagogies don't end there. First, both the New Criticism and the Common Core are far-reaching. An estimated 597,940 copies of *Understanding Poetry* were published between 1936 and 1975, with its impact most forcefully felt through its first two editions (Golding 1995:105); the Common Core had been adopted by forty-six states and Washington, DC, as of 2013.[8] Second, both pedagogies insist on the existence of objectivity and, by extension, objective readings. Third, both pedagogies eschew the role of feeling when reading and interpreting. First described by New Critics W. K. Wimsatt Jr. and M. C. Beardsley (1949:21) as the "affective fallacy," the New Critics believed that affect is "another convenient detour" around "objective criticism" that wrongly underscores a text's "psychological effects" and "ends in impressionism and relativism." Far less eloquently, David Coleman (2011:10), a lead writer and architect of the Common Core, defended its emphasis on argument and objectivity (and implicit stance against personal writing) by saying "as you grow up in this world, you realize that people don't really give a shit about what you feel or think." Those second and third similarities are the most important to the present discussion because by focusing on objectivity rather than the role of the reader in the composition of meaning, both pedagogies seek to depersonalize—in the name of rigor—what it means to read and to be a reader. Both approaches to reading consist of pedagogies that disconnect the text from the reader, severing the important relationship on which reading depends.

The goal of this chapter, though, is not to disparage these pedagogies but to bring to light a largely unexplored revision Brooks and Warren made to their pedagogy, which allowed them to recast the student-text relationship and ultimately reconnect these entities. In its exploration of this remarkable revision that arguably depends on theories of reading that will later become known as "reader-response theory," this chapter lays the theoretical groundwork for the following chapters and serves as a touchstone for the pedagogical revisions and interventions I call for therein.

UNDERSTANDING POETRY, 2ND EDITION: REVISIONS THAT RECOGNIZE THE READER

According to Brooks and Warren's (1950:xxi) correspondences and the preface in the second edition of *Understanding Poetry*, part of the work of the second edition was to make their pedagogy—and the reading practices it sought to foster—more explicit and expansive. I would argue that one of these revisions includes where their pedagogy stands in relation to what they called "message-hunting," a problematic reading practice in which they noticed their students engaging. In the introduction to the first edition of *Understanding Poetry*, Brooks and Warren (1938:12) tell students that "it is highly necessary, if one is to understand poetry[,] to take up some of these typical misreadings," the first of which they call "message-hunting": " 'Message-hunting'—the business of looking only for the statement of an idea which the reader thinks he can apply profitably to his own conduct—is one of the most ordinary forms of [misreading]."

They go on to explain that "the fact that we have just an idea in itself is not enough to make a poem, even when the idea may be a worthy one. The neglect of this principle causes frequent misunderstandings and misreadings of poems" (Brooks and Warren 1938:12). The postscript in the second edition also addresses this approach and includes the following discussion on the dangers of this reading practice: "The moral attitudes [the poem] embodies are, for instance, as deeply involved in the technical ordering of the poem as they are in any statement the poem may make. In fact, they are more deeply involved in the technical ordering. The meaning of the poem is, finally, in the kind of being the poem has and not in any particular statement (taken abstractly) that it may make" (Brooks and Warren 1950:xxv). In other words, Brooks and Warren are most interested in the ontological nature of the poem, "the kind of being the poem has," rather than in what the readers think the poem might teach them. Like the Common Core's commitment to "shif[t] the focus of literacy instruction to center on careful examination of the text itself" (Coleman and Pimentel 2012:1), the New Criticism's reading pedagogy was developed as well to shift students' "misreadings" toward more objective, "accurate" readings.

Rehearsing the New Criticism's well-known theories, the above excerpt's privileging of the poem over the reader is not nearly as surprising as the exercises in the second edition of *Understanding Poetry*, which mark an unexpected departure from the New Critical pedagogy. These exercises foreground the reader by calling on that which the student-readers bring with them, namely, an investment in message-hunting. In other words, the second edition recognizes the reader's role in reading in a way that complicates and potentially challenges the impersonal and objective reading approaches for which the New Critics are largely remembered. Moreover, not only does the second edition recognize the reader, but it recognizes all the student-reader brings with her to the reading experience. This was clearly uncharacteristic of the New Critics' text-centric understandings of reading and far more along the lines of how their contemporary, scholar Louise Rosenblatt, described what happens when one reads. In her own literary criticism from the same period, Rosenblatt (1983:30) described how readers' "personality traits, memories of past events, present needs and preoccupations, a particular mood of the moment, and a particular physical condition" impacted meaning. Although writing at the same time as the New Critics, Rosenblatt's scholarship, first published in 1938, was largely ignored until it was recovered in the 1970s as part of the reader-response movement.

Brooks and Warren's recognition of these influences on meaning is particularly visible in the early chapters of the textbook, since they contained what Brooks and Warren called narrative and implied narrative poems, which are potentially more likely to elicit "message-hunting." In the first edition, Bryant's "To a Waterfowl" is followed by a single exercise: "Compare the statement of the relation of man and bird in this poem with that made in 'The Robin' . . . Is the application made too directly in this poem? How much of the force of the poem depends on the success of description in the first six stanzas?" (Brooks and Warren 1938:189, 191). Although their question regarding the application being "made too directly" might lead one to think about the moral or didactic undertones of the poem, Brooks and Warren (1950:86) make their point far more explicit in the second edition: "Is the 'lesson' that the bird impresses upon the man's heart presented to the reader dramatically, so that the reader, participating imaginatively in the man's experience, also participates in the meaning of the experience? Or is the lesson 'preached' to the reader? (Note that the matter at issue is not whether the message is or is not a true one, nor is it whether a poet may not properly make use of bold and direct statement; it is rather whether the method of presentation used here is effective and appropriate in this particular poem)."

Similar revisions are prevalent in the exercises accompanying Housman's "Hell Gate." The two questions following the poem in the first edition are: "1. What is the implied relation between the speaker and the sentry?" and "2. Since the poem is a fantasy, what is the intention of the narrative?" (Brooks and Warren 1938:149). In the second edition, the poem is accompanied by five detailed questions, the fifth of which is the following: "Does this poem have a message? Is the poem offensively 'moralizing,' making its point too patly? If not, try to indicate [as] specifically as you can what keeps the poem from appearing solemnly moralistic" (Brooks and Warren 1950:64). In these revised exercises, which are indicative of a pattern of revision in the second edition, Brooks and Warren's elaboration includes the directive to locate the moral. In fact, this emerges as a necessary step prior to students' determining "whether the method of presentation used here is effective and appropriate in this particular poem" (Brooks 1945).

Despite this seemingly contradictory aspect of their pedagogy, I would argue that in comparing the first and second editions of *Understanding Poetry*, we see Brooks and Warren revising their pedagogy so that it does not outright reject a reading practice in which they noticed their students engaging but uses it to teach students how to think on a higher, more complicated plane. Brooks and Warren have begun to think about readers and what they bring to what Rosenblatt called the "transaction" between text and reader. In other words, Brooks and Warren seem open to Rosenblatt's (1983:28) theory that "any literary work gains its significance from the way in which the minds and emotions of particular readers respond to the verbal stimuli offered by the text." In the case of message-hunting, the reader brings an approach that is not in line with Brooks and Warren's pedagogy. Still, Brooks and Warren ended up embracing students' tendency to "message-hunt" as a means to completing the more rigorous critical work they expected of students.

RETHINKING THE READER IN THE COMMON CORE

One of the most fundamental aspects of the Common Core that needs to be rethought—and Brooks and Warren's own revisions might serve as a model—is how the Common Core defines the student-reader. A foundational element that has infused literary study since at least the 1970s, but one the Common Core largely ignores, is that the reader plays a role in the construction of meaning. Despite the Common Core's disregard of the reader, as compositionist and rhetorical historian Patricia Harkin (2005:413) points out, this conception of reading has become normalized and "simply assumed in every aspect of our work." She explains further, "Readers make meaning: readers—and not only authors—engage in an active process of production-in-use in which texts of all kinds—stories, poems, plays, buildings, films, TV ads, clothes, body piercings—are received by their audiences not as a repository of stable meaning but as an invitation to make it" (Harkin 2005:413). Yet the Common Core's conception of reading is an unfortunate throwback to a time wherein texts were situated as stable repositories of meaning and, by extension, teachers were cast as the masters and safeguards of these meanings. In the *Revised Publisher's Criteria for the Common Core State Standards* (Coleman and Pimentel 2012:1), the "text itself" is consistently prioritized over the reader: "At the heart of these criteria are instructions for shifting the focus of literacy instruction to center on careful examination of the text itself . . . the standards focus on students reading closely to draw evidence and knowledge from the text . . . .the criteria make plain that developing students' prowess at drawing knowledge from the text itself is the point of reading; reading well means gaining the maximum insight or knowledge possible from each source." This excerpt does not describe students as active participants in the creation of knowledge or insight but as scavengers who must "draw" knowledge and "gain" insight from the text where this knowledge and insight is contained.

The Common Core ELA standards (National Governors Association 2010) themselves also remove the individual reader (and how readers make meaning) from the equation by foregrounding the text and blatantly neglecting to describe how readers' experiences and backgrounds necessarily affect the interpretive process. The Anchor Standards for Reading are listed as follows:

1. Read closely to determine what the text says explicitly and to make logical inferences from it; cite specific textual evidence

when writing or speaking to support conclusions drawn from the text.

2. Determine central ideas or themes of a text and analyze their development; summarize the key supporting details and ideas.

3. Analyze how and why individuals, events, or ideas develop and interact over the course of a text.

4. Interpret words and phrases as they are used in a text, including determining technical, connotative, and figurative meanings, and analyze how specific word choices shape meaning or tone.

5. Analyze the structure of texts, including how specific sentences, paragraphs, and larger portions of the text (e.g., a section, chapter, scene, or stanza) relate to each other and the whole.

6. Assess how point of view or purpose shapes the content and style of a text (National Governors Association 2010).

I wonder what tools students are relying on—if not other reading experiences, lived experience, and background knowledge (all derided by the CCSS)—to read the text explicitly, make logical inferences, determine central themes, summarize, analyze, and interpret. Furthermore, the repetition of the phrase the "text itself" throughout the *Revised Publisher's Criteria* and the CCSS not only disconnects the students' experiences and backgrounds from the reading process but excludes the reader from the act of reading, as the text is described as totally separate from the reader. Flying in the face of what we have known about reading for at least fifty years (e.g., Haas and Flower 1988; Berthoff 1981a, 1981b; Iser 1978; Salvatori 2002; Blau 2003a)—and an additional twenty-five if you go as far back as Louise Rosenblatt's work, initially published in 1938—the Common Core bases its reading pedagogy on long outdated notions of what it means to read.

Instead of pretending that this understanding of reading hasn't existed for decades, why not—taking a cue from Brooks and Warren's revision—consider doing what they did, namely, recognizing and using what student-readers bring to the text even if it's not an end in itself? Brooks and Warren ultimately relied on students' default reading practices (i.e., message-hunting) even though they didn't agree with them. Current teachers might use students' personal experiences and backgrounds—as they have been doing for years—as a means to get them thinking in more critical ways about the texts they encounter.

Rigor—the goal of both the New Criticism and the Common Core—need not be cast in opposition to these more reader-oriented practices. Describing how it is "fashionable these days to see 'rigor' and 'grit' and stamina as the key characteristics of a strong learner" (Newkirk 2017:184), literacy expert Thomas Newkirk (2017:185–86) notes that these "qualities of persistence are really by-products (or perhaps the outer appearance) of a capacity for sustained engagement . . . We become more effective thinkers if we can keep an object of attention alive and moving. We don't stop with the first impression; we don't give up when we meet difficulty. We can ask questions, make associations, explore alternatives, name our confusion, ask how we can resolve it." It is this valuing of sustained engagement, of reading as a recursive act, and of this mindful pose that sometimes gets lost in contemporary iterations of reader-response theory. Harkin (2005:419) reminds us that reader-response theory was characterized by "very considerable theoretical sophistication," but as time went on it "came to be associated, almost exclusively, with pedagogy . . . as compositionists sought to use reader-response theory to teach students to read difficult texts." The "touchy-feely, anything-goes" approach that reader-response theory has come to represent is an unfair characterization that undermines the complexity associated with reader-oriented theories. By obscuring the complexity of the reading process, the Common Core, unfortunately, severs the important relationship between the reader and the text, wherein the reader acts as co-creator. In so doing, the student-teacher relationship becomes tenuous as well, as teachers are put in the position of having to tell students to pretend that their experiences, cultures, and backgrounds are not impacting their reading.

There are ways, though, that instructors can honor what students bring to the reading process. There is a long history of activities like freewriting and journaling—two common first steps in the writing process—that ask students to draw on their experiences and backgrounds to ultimately develop a piece of writing that moves beyond the personal, even though these early steps often traffic in the personal. Reading research (e.g., Smagorinsky 2001; Cioffi 2005; Cody 1996; Mutnick 1998) and reader-response theory suggest that the same is true about reading—students who begin with personally inflected reading responses can be prompted—often more successfully than students who don't—to use what they always already bring with them to ultimately move their thinking to a more critical place.

Specifically, encouraging students to reflect on their reading processes in a reading journal by commenting on how and why they think they arrived at the reading they did reinserts them, the readers, into the equation and suggests that "what lies within the four corners of the text" (Coleman and Pimentel 2012:4) may define where the text ends but does not define how reading works. Reflective exercises help students understand that they don't randomly arrive at interpretations, but they are inflected by a range of factors. Teachers might also focus on the range of *different* readings and interpretations (rather than coaxing students toward one) that students have developed. This activity highlights that reading is dependent on more than the text. While some readings will likely be more tenable than others—an important part of the discussion in and of itself—teachers could focus their time on the why (we arrive at different readings) and the how (that happens) of reading rather than on the content, the what. This reflective work has the potential to help sharpen students' abilities to read without privileging the text at the expense of the reader.

None of the reflective activities described above are revolutionary, but they are first steps toward (1) reinserting the reader (and all the reader brings with her) in the process of reading, (2) giving students the agency the Common Core's reading pedagogy denies them, and (3) preparing them for the metacognitive work they will be expected to do in college.

FROM THE COMMON CORE TO COLLEGE-LEVEL READING

This meta-cognitive approach to reading, largely absent from the Common Core, helps define what it means to be a college-level reader. Alice Horning (2014:51), a leading expert on reading and college-level reading in particular, has declared: "Our goals are clear: moving students toward expert awareness of the texts they read, developing metacognitive assessment of them, and developing their skills in analysis, synthesis, evaluation, application in every course, every term, digital and traditional, high school and college." Testing students' reflective practices, including student-readers' awareness and meta-cognitive assessments, is clearly more difficult than the text-centric questions the Common Core prepares students to answer. As Chris Gilbert (2014:32) points out, the standards' valuing of the text over the reader is no accident: "It is no coincidence that the text-centric analysis promoted by the standards readily lends itself to standardized assessment. These tests do not prompt students to connect text to life, or to consider how language has informed their view of the world," even though studies show that students struggle with this (Jolliffe and Harl 2008). I would add that it is also not a coincidence that Coleman—a lead writer, architect, and the face of the CCSS—is also the president and chief executive officer of the College Board, the testing company that owns the Advanced Placement (AP) exams and the SAT exam. In fact, Coleman recently redesigned the SAT so it is linked to the CCSS. The point is that we need to push back against text-centric pedagogies that lend themselves to standardized assessments developed by someone who benefits from those very standardized assessments. We must instead focus on what it is that research on reading indicates our students need.

Simply accepting the characterization of the reader that the Common Core posits could have serious consequences. In the short term, although the Common Core strives to "prepare students for college and the workforce" (Coleman and Pimentel 2012), it potentially takes away students' agency by dismissing them, their experiences, and their backgrounds. Horning (2014), who thinks of college students as "apprentices on the journey between novice and expert," has underscored the importance of students' experiences and backgrounds to the college reading experience. She writes that "apprentice readers should engage in dialogue among texts and authors, be engaged in talk about texts, and draw upon their own experiences and understanding to reach higher levels of reading comprehension" (Horning 2014:48). If students are arriving at college from high schools wherein they have been forbidden to draw on their own experiences and understandings, per the Common Core standards, then they will actually be less prepared for college than were previous generations.

While worrisome in and of itself, this lack of preparation may not be the worst consequence. As the Common Core dismisses the role of the reader, it simultaneously "diminishes the concern with the human meaningfulness" of the reading process (Rosenblatt 1983:29). Rosenblatt (1983:40) explains, "The ability to understand and sympathize with others reflects the multiple nature of the human being, his potentiality for many more selves and kinds of experiences than anyone could begin to express." The Common Core has not only encouraged less reading of literature—in favor of informational texts—thereby reducing students' opportunities to understand and empathize, but by ignoring the reader altogether, the Common Core has dehumanized students and, as Daniel E. Ferguson (2013–14) points out, silenced their voices. Others agree. Sheridan Blau, whose widely influential book *The Literature Workshop* (2003a) and other scholarship (2003b) details the dispositions that will help students become strong readers, describes the Common Core's prioritization of informational texts over literature as a "misguided prejudice among school administrators across the country against literature" (Blau 2014:45). Literacy expert Thomas Newkirk (2013:1) has characterized the standards as presenting an "inhumanly fractured model of what goes on in deep reading," and Jason Endacott and Christian Z. Goering (2014:90) have noted that "our children have become akin to new products some 'edu-corporation' wants to research and develop before bringing to market. Not surprisingly, the product reflects exactly what big business values in its workers—emphasis on analysis, argument, and specialization—at the potential expense of beauty, empathy, personal reflection, and humanity." The Common Core's misplaced values are perhaps most visible in the increasing educational inequalities, which assessments of the Core have corroborated, as schools with poorer students have become what journalist and educator Alan Singer (2014) calls "giant test-prep factories, enriching publishers" but ignoring students' needs.

Without being an alarmist, it is worth considering what this dehumanization might mean not just for students but for our culture. As Robert Scholes (2002) has pointed out, students have trouble considering themselves and their experiences in relation to and—more importantly—in contrast to those of others: "After 11 September 2001 we have begun to learn, perhaps, that this deficiency is serious." He goes on to describe English teachers' responsibility to help our students develop reading practices "in which strength comes, paradoxically, from subordinating one's own thoughts temporarily to the views and values of another person" (Scholes 2002:167–68). Not only does the Common Core refuse to acknowledge student-readers as people with personality traits and legitimate experiences, it misses opportunities to help students connect, understand, and empathize with others—whether characters in a novel or an author of an op-ed. In the end, students are robbed of their voices, agency, and any sort of dialogue about meaning that should characterize classroom discussions.

As Louise Rosenblatt (1983) has pointed out, this dialogue plays several important roles that extend far beyond the classroom: "The emotional character of the student's response to literature offers an opportunity to develop *the ability to think rationally within an emotionally colored context*." Furthermore, she continues, "The teaching situation in which a group of students and a teacher exchange views and stimulate one another toward clearer understanding can contribute greatly to such habits of reflection" (Rosenblatt 1983:227–28, emphasis in original), including the "development of critical and self-critical reading, essential to citizens of a democracy" (Rosenblatt 1983:180). With their reductive understanding of reading, the CCSS do not allow reading (and especially the reading of literature) to play its role as "a potential means of developing social understanding" (Rosenblatt 1983:237). Moreover, with the CCSS' stance against personal response, students are not able to offer "emotional responses—the starting point for intelligent behavior" (Rosenblatt 1983:238).

The CCSS, or Coleman's thinly veiled admonition of reader-response theory that outright rejects the role of emotion in reading, miss the complexities and nuances of that theory, which Rosenblatt (2005:xxx), in an interview with Nicholas Karolides, described as follows:

> If the reading transaction leads students to talk and write about specifically personal matters, that is probably a good sign, especially early in the transition to this approach. But in these days of what seems, in print and TV, almost a confessional mania, the danger is to think that the job is done, that that is the final goal. Personal response, to my mind, has to do with the entire process of response to the text. Students don't need necessarily to write about Uncle Bob, they need to be free to draw on ideas, expectations, attitudes that are the residue of having known Uncle Bob. That's what the importance of the personal aspect adds up to—freely drawing on what the signs stir up in the reservoir of past experience in order to make personally significant new meanings. That's simply basic to all aspects of evoking and reflecting on meaning—such as the choice of stance, reflection on the evoked experience from a broader perspective, recognition of personal bias—basic for growth.

Rosenblatt's description of "confessional mania" is even more relevant in today's digital and social-media-driven world. This confessional mania seems to be one of the driving forces behind the reading pedagogy of the CCSS that denies the role of personal response altogether in reading. But in this excerpt, Rosenblatt reminds us that responding to a text by simply talking and writing about personal matters is not the ultimate goal of reader-response approaches to texts. Instead, it is an initial step in the process of constructing meaning, much like message-hunting in the second edition of *Understanding Poetry*.

Rosenblatt's clarification of reader-response theory's investment in holistic understandings of reading also suggests the
relationship she imagines between literary study and democracy.
The former allows readers to "develop the imaginative capacity
to put themselves in the place of others—a capacity essential in
a democracy, where we need to rise above narrow self-interest
and envision the broader human consequences of political
decisions." Rosenblatt (2005:xxxiii) continues, "If I have been
involved with the development of the ability to read critically
across the whole intellectual spectrum, it is because such abilities are particularly important for citizens in a democracy."

As suggested earlier in this chapter, Rosenblatt's theory of
reading, which is overtly connected to the needs of a democracy
(rather than just to college and career preparation, as are the
CCSS), is not just an alternative to the theory of reading that
informs the CCSS. Instead, it is a—if not the—foundational theory of reading that continues to inform reading research and literary studies in the fields of English, education, and psychology,
among others. Moreover, Rosenblatt's theories bear returning
to because we now know—from the studies detailed below—
that the students who have been subject to the Common Core
still do not seem prepared to critically read the texts or the
world around them.

STUDENTS' READING ABILITIES

While the architects of the CCSS may have us look at the Common
Core's sanctioned assessment tools—PARCC (Partnership for
Assessment of Readiness for College and Careers) and SBAC
(Smarter Balanced Assessment Consortium)—to assess how
students are doing in light of this curriculum, these tools have
been the source of much debate and have seen a sharp decline
in the number of schools that use them (Gewertz 2016). First,
these assessments potentially pose a conflict of interest because
they are financially supported by those who support the CCSS,
including the Bill and Melinda Gates Foundation. They have
been described as inadequately aligned with the CCSS (Law

2016) and have been used as pawns in both local and national politics (Heyboer 2015; Jochim and McGuinn 2016). In light of these entanglements, I turn my attention to a range of both small- and large-scale studies that offer insight into students' critical reading abilities.

The SAT Verbal/Critical Reading Portion has shown a steep decline in students' reading abilities over the last several decades. Despite criticisms of the test, its long history allows for comparisons over time, comparisons that reveal that "in 2015, the average score on the SAT verbal test was near historic lows" ("Performance on SAT Verbal/Critical Reading and Writing Exams" 2016). Like SAT scores, ACT scores are also used for admission and placement. Recent scores on the ACT Reading Portion from approximately 2 million students nationwide also indicated a decline. As Horning (2017b:3) points out, in ACT's 2015 report, "Forty-six percent of students hit ACT's cutoff score of 22 on the Reading [Portion], needed to be 'successful' in college. ACT defines success as having a 2.0 GPA and returning for a second year of study. It's worth noting that this result is a decline from the 51% who hit the cutoff score as reported in 2006, when ACT did a big study of students' reading performance."

Although focused on students' source-based *writing* habits, the Citation Project, a multi-institutional empirical research project, revealed disturbing data about students' reading habits. Rebecca Moore Howard, Tricia Serviss, and Tanya K. Rodrigue (2010:189) found that students focused on a very limited amount of text while summarizing the sources they used in their writing, raising questions about "whether students understand the sources they are citing." Students avoided working with the larger ideas in the sources, often constructing arguments "from isolated sentences pulled from sources" (Howard, Serviss, and Rodrigue 2010:189). These and related findings have led Sandra Jamieson (2013), a member of the research team, to conclude that "students lack the critical reading and thinking skills necessary to engage with the ideas of others and write papers reflecting that engagement in any discipline."

STUDENTS' DIGITAL READING ABILITIES

Although digital natives, students' online reading habits are equally poor. In their study of just over 200 college students, Ericka Menchen-Trevino and Eszter Hargittai (2011) found that students largely did not understand Wikipedia's editing process (despite using it regularly), which makes them particularly susceptible to believing whatever they read on the site. James P. Purdy's (2012) study of 523 students' reading habits indicated that students choose sources based on their ease of use as opposed to the relevance to their subject. Relevance was, in fact, one of the least important criteria students reported using for choosing an online source (Purdy 2012).

A large-scale study titled Project SAILS (Standardized Assessment of Information Literacy Skills) lends additional validity to these smaller studies. A standardized test (now owned by Carrick Enterprises) designed by faculty and librarians at Kent State University and based on the American Library Association of College and Research Librarians' Information Literacy Standards for Higher Education, Project SAILS tests students' information literacy skills, including how well students access, locate, evaluate, understand and use online information. As Horning (2012:177) points out, only 50 percent of about 6,400 high school, community college, and four-year college and university students were deemed to have the essential information literacy skills. These findings, of course, raise questions about students' most fundamental abilities to successfully understand online information.

Most recently, a similarly large-scale study of middle-schoolers through college students conducted by the Stanford History Education Group (2016) found that students are not adept at evaluating—or reading—the credibility of online sources, despite the standards' commitment to digital literacy. The study, titled *Evaluating Information: The Cornerstone of Civic Online Reasoning*, which included 7,804 students from schools (both under-resourced and well-resourced) across twelve states, as well as students from six universities, sought to gauge students' capacities for "civic online reasoning." Detailing their methods, the researchers explain in the Executive Summary:

We did not design our exercises to shake out a grade or make hairsplitting distinctions between a "good" and a "better" answer. Rather, we sought to establish a reasonable bar, a level of performance we hoped was within reach of most middle school, high school, and college students. For example, we would hope that middle school students could distinguish an ad from a news story. By high school, we would hope that students reading about gun laws would notice that a chart came from a gun owners' political action committee. And, in 2016, we would hope college students, who spend hours each day online, would look beyond a .org URL and ask who's behind a site that presents only one side of a contentious issue. *But in every case and at every level, we were taken aback by students' lack of preparation.* (Stanford History Education Group 2016:4, emphasis added)

Overall, the middle-schoolers, high schoolers, and college students were ill-prepared to successfully complete their assigned tasks. The Executive Summary explains that "more than 80% of the middle-schoolers believed that the native advertisement, identified by the words 'sponsored content,' was a real news story. Some students even mentioned that it was sponsored content but still believed that it was a news article" (Stanford History Education Group 2016:10). Across all grade levels, the high school students who participated in the study "were captivated by the photograph" of the misshapen flowers growing near a power plant that they were asked to view. These students "relied on [only the photo] to evaluate the trustworthiness of the post, ignoring key details, such as the source (none was named) of the photo. Less than 20% of [these] students constructed 'Mastery' responses, or responses that questioned the source of the post or the source of the photo. On the other hand, nearly 40% of students argued that the post provided strong evidence because it presented pictorial evidence about conditions near the power plant" (Stanford History Education Group 2016:17).

The participating college students had trouble evaluating tweets, a form of social media with which they regularly engage: "Only a few students noted that the tweet was based on a poll conducted by a professional polling firm and explained why this would make the tweet a stronger source of information. Similarly, less than a third of students fully explained how the political agendas of MoveOn.org and the Center for American Progress might influence the content of the tweet. Many students made broad statements about the limitations of polling or the dangers of social media content instead of investigating the particulars of the organizations involved in this tweet" (Stanford History Education Group 2016:23).

In all of these cases, all three populations failed to adeptly read the online information, despite the Common Core's commitment to helping students "integrate and evaluate information presented in diverse media and formats, including visually, quantitatively, and orally" (National Governors Association Center for Best Practices and Council of Chief State School Officers). Instead, these students accepted what was before them: they read the sponsored content as a news article; they read the photograph of the flower as pictorial evidence, despite no mention of its source; and they ignored the significance of the credible polling firm behind the information shared in the tweet.

Brian White has suggested that students' difficulties are connected to the CCSS's emphasis on revering texts. White (2015:33) points out that Coleman describes literature as "'the master class' for which he has 'a certain reverence,' and himself as the 'teacher and the student and the servant of it.'" With its repetition of the phrase "the text itself" and its admonition to students to stick within the "four corners of the text," this reverence would seem to apply to informational texts as well, or at least those sanctioned by the CCSS, which favor historical nonfiction over biographies (i.e., mere stories). These studies suggest that the standards' emphasis on text-based evidence, which would seem to be of great import within a post-truth climate, has yet to prepare students to read the texts that surround them. In fact, because the CCSS encourage students to revere texts, it really shouldn't come as a surprise that students in this study were not inclined to question the texts (and the evidence therein) placed before them. The standards' text-centric, narrow approach to reading does not prepare students to engage texts in deep ways—to question, challenge, and maybe even seek to disprove them. Instead, the CCSS teach students to revere texts.

This outdated approach to reading is indicative, some would say, of a more generally outdated education system that has not evolved alongside technological advances that make different demands on readers. Professor of education and history at Stanford University, as well as the lead author of the Stanford study mentioned above, Sam Wineburg contends in an interview with Kelly McEvers (2016) that education has "not caught up to the way [online] sources of information are influencing the kinds of conceptions that we develop on a day-to-day basis." Wineburg notes that in "many schools there are internet filters that direct students to previously vetted sites and reliable sources of information." But "what happens," he asks, "when they leave school and they take out their phone and they look at their Twitter feed? How do they become prepared to make the choices about what to believe, what to forward, what to post to their friends when they've [been] given no practice in doing those kinds of things in school?" "Consequently," he continues, "what we see is a rash of fake news going on that people pass on without thinking. And we really can't blame young people because we've never taught them to do otherwise" (McEvers 2016).[9] The findings from all the studies detailed above seem to corroborate Wineburg's description of the education system as failing its students in this area. Thus, we must ask ourselves: how can we do better?

ADDITIONAL PEDAGOGICAL INTERVENTIONS

In addition to the reflective assignments described earlier in this chapter, other pedagogical interventions can help students read, understand, and evaluate online sources. The researchers who conducted the Stanford study have released the reading assignments they used in that study so instructors can incorporate these vetted activities into their courses. That is certainly a place to start. Just as Project SAILS used the Association of

College and Research Libraries (ACRL) information literacy standards to test students' capacities to understand and use online texts, so can instructors refer to these newly revised standards and to their own campus and school librarians as they imagine their pedagogical goals and the assignments they will create for students.

The *Framework for Success in Postsecondary Writing* (2011), developed collaboratively by representatives from the Council of Writing Program Administrators (CWPA), the National Council of Teachers of English (NCTE), and the National Writing Project (NWP), is also an important resource. The framework lists eight habits of mind—curiosity, openness, engagement, creativity, persistence, responsibility, flexibility, and meta-cognition—described as "ways of approaching learning" that are "essential for success in college writing." Particularly if one imagines how these habits also correspond to reading, writing's counterpart in the construction of meaning (Carillo 2017b; Horning 2017a), these habits, as Patrick Sullivan (2012:547) has pointed out, direct attention to "qualities" rather than target test scores or some other criteria. These (and other) habits of mind are described in Blau's (2003b:19) scholarship as *performative literacy*, "knowledge that enables readers to activate and use all the other forms of knowledge that are required for the exercise of anything like a critical or disciplined literacy." Blau (2003b:19) identifies "seven traits as constitutive of performative literacy, each one associated with actions and dispositions that distinguish more competent from less competent readers." More recently, Richard E. Miller and Ann Jurecic's unorthodox textbook *Habits of the Creative Mind* offers another valuable resource that shifts attention toward the importance of literacy instruction in helping students cultivate specific habits of mind.

THE TEACHER'S ROLE IN FORGING AHEAD

As we think about developing pedagogies that meet our students' literacy needs, we must pay close attention to the role we assign to instructors. As Richard E. Miller (2016:154) points out, prior to the internet, it was the teacher's job to provide content and knowledge as "the professor was once the library's mobile memory drive": "When information was scarce, schooling involved getting the information out of the library and into the students' heads, with the professor doing double duty as the conduit for the flow of information and the quality control manager." But now that information is "ubiquitous, it is no longer possible to master a content area . . . the professor's role in this new digital learning environment is not to play the part of the master of content; it is to be the master of resourcefulness. In this role, the teacher models how to think in the face of an endless torrent of information" (Miller 2016:155). We need to think about what this means for reading since despite the paradigm shift Miller describes, the CCSS privilege the text's content—as accessed through a very New Critical kind of close reading—and locate teachers as masters of that content. As Miller convincingly argues, this role no longer makes much sense.

CONCLUDING THOUGHTS

Students' lack of preparation for college is perhaps not nearly as significant as their lack of preparation for participating in a democracy. In fact, the findings from the Stanford study led the members of its research team to conclude that "democracy is threatened by the ease at which disinformation about civic issues is allowed to spread and flourish" (Stanford History Education Group 2016:5).[10] The term *disinformation* is crucial here because it reminds us that an informed citizenry is not enough to sustain a democracy. There is plenty of information to go around. Citizens in information-rich cultures like our own must be taught ways of reading and understanding all that surrounds them, particularly in such a "cacophonous democracy" (McEvers 2016). Citizens must be reflective. They must be taught to question and challenge texts rather than just revere them. They must be taught to question themselves and their biases. As I have suggested throughout, Louise Rosenblatt's foundational theory of reading reminds us what this looks like in the classroom and provides a much-needed alternative to the reading pedagogy detailed in the CCSS.

Maybe it's the inability to remove ourselves from the contemporary moment that leads us to believe that something is happening now that has never happened before, but democracy really does feel like it's at stake. Our students are simply not receiving the reading instruction that prepares them for college or for being active and thoughtful participants in our democracy. More than three decades ago, Robert Scholes (1986:15) lamented: "The students who come to us now exist in the most manipulative culture human beings have ever experienced. They are bombarded with signs, with rhetoric, from their daily awakenings until their troubled sleep." "The worst thing we can do," warned Scholes (1986:16), "is to foster in them an attitude of reverence before texts."

As the standards enact what Scholes deems "the worst thing we can do" by fostering in students a reverence for texts without recognizing the potentially disastrous consequences of this way of reading in a post-truth culture, educators are uniquely positioned to mitigate these consequences, and they can do so in some of the ways I describe in this chapter and throughout this book.

3

CULTIVATING EMPATHIC READING, READERS, AND RESEARCHERS

This chapter recovers some of the scholarship from what has been called the "affective turn" in composition to argue for its relevance in today's divisive climate. Drawing on this scholarship, as well as on scientific research on cognition and emotion, this chapter argues for highlighting the affective components of composing meaning, aspects the Common Core State Standards, discussed in chapter 2, largely reject. Scholarship from this period situates emotion within the realm of rhetoric but goes beyond more traditional applications of emotion in classical rhetoric, such as audience-centered rhetorical appeals. By considering the rhetoricity of emotion, these scholars have laid the groundwork for imagining a response to the current climate that expands composition's dependence on largely rational epistemologies. Moreover, recent scientific studies that locate emotion as intertwined with rationality—rather than separate from it or as a threat to it—further suggest the value of attending to how our students' emotions affect how they construct meaning as they read.

Beginning with an overview of the affective turn in composition, this chapter then considers the benefits of incorporating attention to empathy in writing classrooms. This chapter demonstrates how my pedagogy inadvertently foreclosed opportunities for students to acknowledge and reflect on how their emotions inform their beliefs and, therefore, their reading practices. In reflecting on my own pedagogy I consider what introducing emotion, specifically the concept of empathy, might offer the composition classroom. From there, the chapter expands

DOI: 10.7330/9781607327912.c003

outward to argue for making empathy more central to the research we conduct, particularly in participant-focused studies.

REVISITING THE AFFECTIVE TURN IN COMPOSITION

In the last few years of the twentieth century and into the twenty-first century, we witnessed what is now called the "affective turn" in composition.[11] The affective turn is largely thought of as a response to the political turn in composition, which as Laura Micciche (2002:436) points out was "slow to address the emotional contexts of teaching and learning." A challenge to theories that focused only on rational inquiry, the scholarship that emerges from composition's affective turn considers what other means, including those affective means, are available for inquiring into social and power structures, identity, and the other issues the tools of critical pedagogies promised to help us explore. "We want to suggest," write Dale Jacobs and Micciche (2003:2) in the introduction to their edited collection *A Way to Move*, "that emotion . . . enables and disables change. In particular, we are interested in emotion's capacity to construct a culture of movement in opposition to one of ossification." In this scholarship, which builds on feminist critiques of emotion as irrational, emotion is defined as both socially constructed and experienced, as opposed to biologically determined.[12] By removing emotion from the individual sphere, denaturalizing it, and underscoring its connections to cognition and rationality, these scholars pushed against the "Western cultural bias against affect as a serious topic of academic interest" (McLeod 1997:5). Among other salient topics, scholars studied the overlooked but complicated role of emotion in Aristotle's writing (Quandahl 2003), the narrowly audience-centered definitions of emotion throughout composition textbooks and rhetoric anthologies (Micciche 2007), and the emotional dimensions of teaching, learning, and disciplinary structures.

The affective turn also brought to the fore arguments for more holistic literacy instruction as well as scholarship. Compositionists writing during the affective turn maintain that because the whole body and its myriad functions are involved in learning, we must consider far more than students' cognitive functions (as they are usually narrowly defined) when theorizing literacy pedagogies. Moreover, their scholarship often modeled this method by collapsing barriers between "academic" and "personal writing." These arguments are reminiscent of those made by Ann E. Berthoff (1981a, 198ab), Jim W. Corder (1985), and James Moffett (1968), among others. At that time, Berthoff (1981b:64) pointed out the problem with the "false dichotomy" between imagination and cognition, pleading that "reclaiming the imagination is necessary because the positivists have consigned it to something called the affective domain in contradiction to the cognitive domain."

Also during this early period, which informs the more recent affective turn and the current renewed focus on affect and embodied literacies, psychologist Carl Rogers's work on interpersonal communication, especially his scholarship on nondirective counseling practices, was adapted by compositionists for use in the teaching of argument. Richard Young, Alton L. Becker, and Kenneth L. Pike (1970) "attempted to tease out the argumentative aspect of Rogers' theories and apply them to persuasion and writing" (Kearney 2009:168). Despite the recognition of what some see as a "giant leap" from therapeutic practices to pedagogical practices (Corder 1985; Kearney 2009; Teich 1987; Ede 1984), this did "little to discourage the association of Rogerian principles with rhetoric and writing pedagogy" (Kearney 2009:168) in the 1970s and 1980s. Many scholars, including Maxine Hairston (1976) and Andrea A. Lunsford (1979), for example, reported incorporating "Rogerian Rhetoric" into their teaching because it allowed them to explore the roles of emotion and listening in argument.

DEFINING EMPATHY

Before detailing how the concept of empathy might become more central to our work in composition, it is important to define empathy. Definitions of empathy abound, a fact that itself has been the focus of a great deal of scholarship (e.g., Coplan 2011; Batson 2009; Lindhé 2016). For the purposes of this chapter, we can begin with Grit Hein and Tania Singer's (2008:154) definition of empathy as "an affective state, caused by sharing of the emotions or sensory states of another person." Empathy, from the German "einfühlung," which translates as "in feeling," is a kind of emotion or, more specifically, a kind of emotion of identification that is experienced *in relation* to something or someone else. Empathy is "having an emotion that is somewhat like the emotion experienced by the target person" (Mar et al. 2011:824). That feeling of empathy is produced by observing or imagining the other's emotion. Moreover, the person who is empathizing recognizes that the other is the source of that emotion. It is that recognition of the source that separates empathy from sympathy, with the latter dependent on a more concrete divide between two people wherein sympathy is understood as a feeling *for* someone rather than a feeling *in*. It is also that *re-cognition* that situates empathy as both cognitive and affective (Decety 2010; Johnson 2012).

Although most often studied within the context of social relationships, empathy has become a key concept for describing what happens during the process of reading literary fiction, particularly because empathy does not necessarily involve the observation of said emotion (in real life) but instead the imagination of that emotion (Mar et al. 2011:824). Oatley (2012:427) explains further: "The fictional work gives us cues as to what happens when each action is performed, and we then experience empathetically (within the simulation of the social world that we are running) the emotions that we would feel in relation to the outcomes of actions as depicted by the author." Many preliminary studies conducted by cognitive psychologists (Johnson 2012; Mar et al. 2011; Kidd and Castano 2013) have supported the hypothesis that fiction does foster empathy in its readers, which makes the Common Core State Standards' elevation of informational texts over literature, particularly in such a divisive climate, that much harder to swallow.

THE INTERDEPENDENCE OF EMOTION AND COGNITION

After decades of debate, cognitive psychologists have also come to believe that empathy and other emotions are not distinct from cognition, a theory that underscores the relevance of attending to students' emotions in the classroom. Previously dismissed as non-rational and a *threat* to rationality, emotion and affect more generally have been studied by scientists using a range of approaches, and these studies have supported this theory of interdependence.

Neurobiologists, for example, maintain that "no brain areas can be designated specifically as 'cognitive' or 'affective.' Although it is the case that subcortical regions are regulated by prefrontal cortical regions," explain neurobiologists Seth Duncan and Lisa Feldman Barrett, "this state of affairs does not inevitably translate into the conclusion that cognitive parts of the brain regulate affective parts of the brain. Instead, it appears that affect is instantiated by a widely distributed, functional network that includes both subcortical regions (typically called 'affective') and anterior frontal regions (traditionally called 'cognitive')" (Duncan and Barrett 2007:1186). Social psychologists have shown how moods affect people's perceptions. Justin Storbeck and Gerald L. Clore (2007) describe Riener, Stefanucci, Proffitt, and Clore's 2003 study in which "participants listened to happy or sad music as they stood at the bottom of a hill . . . Sad mood led to overestimation of the incline on verbal and visual measures . . . the sad individuals were more likely to say that the hill was steeper compared to happy individuals." In addition, clinical psychologists are working toward a "clearer understanding of the connection between cognitive processes and emotional problems" in light of "the successful application of cognitive therapies to affective disorders" (Eich and Schooler 2000:3). And finally, because cognitive psychologists have determined that "emotions are not just physical but evaluative," they call emotions "appraisals" (Oatley and Johnson-Laird 2014:134) and describe their centrality to our existence: "In a world that is not fully predictable, evaluation of the significance of everyday events and of people with whom one interacts makes emotions central to life" (Oatley and Johnson-Laird 2014:134). In other words, emotions play a significant role in how we construct meaning—how we read the world around us, how we judge, and how we make choices. As cognition and emotion are now viewed as "complementary rather than antagonistic processes" (Storbeck and Clore 2007) in the field of psychology, it only follows that other fields, like ours, would recognize that "affect is a potential moderator of all kinds of cognitive operations from perception and attention to implicit learning and implicit associations" (Storbeck and Clore 2007).

If instructors in rhetoric and composition (and those beyond) recognize that cognition and emotion are "inherently integrated" and that "emotional cues regulate cognitive processing" (Storbeck and Clore 2007), we must also believe alongside cognitive psychologists that "there is no such thing as a 'nonaffective thought' and that affect plays a role in perception and cognition, even when people cannot feel its influence" (Duncan and Barrett 2007). Such a scientific theory supports not only the next section's call for reading pedagogies that value students' emotions as integrated aspects of their cognition but this entire chapter's effort to describe how teaching and research in rhetoric and composition might be enriched by the recognition of the interdependence of emotion and cognition.

REVISITING AND REVISING MY PEDAGOGY

The stakes seem higher than ever to help produce "citizens who understand and appreciate the transformative power of listening, who are willing and interested in engaging others with empathy, and whose first response to a complex problem is to read, research, and reflect" (Sullivan 2014:118). Since my early years of teaching I have been looking for ways—to use Robert Scholes's (2002:169) words—to encourage students to put themselves into a text before taking themselves out of it as they compose meaning through the acts of reading and writing. In what follows I revisit two of my own pedagogical strategies for encouraging students to resist the temptation to rush to judgment about texts (and ideas therein) and instead to slow down and dwell a bit in texts with the goal of understanding before critiquing. In revisiting these strategies, I imagine how deliberately attending to students' emotions as they read offers a more productive and comprehensive approach in comparison to my initial approach. In undertaking this work, I hope to model how other instructors might begin to raise questions about the values implicit in their own pedagogies that may foreclose opportunities to attend to the meaning making that occurs in the emotional domain.

In a 2010 article published in *Rhetoric Review* I describe a pedagogy that sought to redirect students' attention away from the argumentative elements of what we were reading, such as claims and evidence, and toward stylistic elements that contribute to a text's meaning. This approach, which involved drawing students' attention to figures of thought—interactional devices or gestures within texts that mark the relationships among participants—offered an antidote to students' narrow way of reading, namely, only for argument and largely to find holes in these arguments. My introduction of this more comprehensive approach to reading might be understood as complementary to efforts to expand more simplistic forms of argumentative writing that continue to circulate, as described by Sullivan (2014). Just as students who are expected to write simplistic, mastery-driven arguments become trapped in a world of stating and defending their positions and opinions, so, too, do students get caught in this immature cognitive stage (Sullivan 2014:59) when they read only for argument, particularly when they define argument in simplistic terms. This oversimplified understanding of argument, I contend in that piece, led to oversimplified readings wherein students mistook complexity for hypocrisy in writing as varied as Virginia Woolf's, Jamaica Kincaid's, and Sven Birkerts's.[13] In that essay I describe the problem and my proposed solution:

> When students characterize these texts and writers [as hypocritical], they have paid exclusive attention to the validity and consistency of argument at the expense of any other elements of the text—including stylistic elements—upon which they might have

commented. It seemed to me that students' rhetoric was impoverished: They didn't know how else to read a text or what to do with a text other than look for the arguments it advances. A valuable mode of reading, reading for argument is not the only way to read and nor is it the only way to conceive of reading's counterpart in the composition process, writing . . . My task became clear: I needed to introduce a richer rhetorical context within which my students could read and write. This context would need to provide the means by which students could learn to recognize and describe—in the service of better understanding and writing—aspects of prose that contribute to a text's meaning. Without the tools or vocabulary to do this work, though, I put my students at a disadvantage. The same way that they were taught how to read for argument, I would need to teach them how to read for these elements, elements that had the potential to open up for them ways of saying more about these texts whose authors were relying on a range of stylistic devices. This richer rhetorical context would provide the means by which students could learn to describe the gestures, moves, and devices that make prose manifest rather than simply the argument it advances . . . A sensitivity to figures of thought, in particular, enables readers and writers to see more clearly the interactive nature of speaking and writing and, more generally, how style functions rhetorically. If language is the unit by which we compose meaning then giving students the resources to attend to the functional dimension of language through stylistic study in theirs and others' writing must not be an afterthought, but a vital and sustained aspect of reading and writing instruction. (Carillo 2010:381–82)

As I read the excerpt now, almost a decade after I wrote it, I am struck by how my solution to students' impoverished ways of reading remains staunchly in the cognitive or rational domain. Although this excerpt—and the piece as a whole—recognizes that students' rhetoric is impoverished, that they didn't know how to read beyond paying exclusive attention to a text's argument, and that they needed a richer rhetorical context in which to read and write, my solution was to "expand" their rhetorical repertoire by giving them more of the same—simply another rationally based method for making sense of the texts before them. Reflecting on this approach, I wonder why I didn't instead encourage them to apply and explore altogether different ways of understanding and knowing—emotionally inflected epistemologies. After all, students' emotions impacted how they read and made sense of these specific texts in the first place, texts that imagine their readers in very particular and complex ways and, as such, often evoke pointed responses from readers. I gave students no real space to acknowledge the emotional component that influenced why they were constructing the meanings they were constructing. I gave them no opportunity to truly expand their rhetorical repertoires to include attention to how texts persuade through modes beyond the rational. As much as the pedagogy described in that piece sought to de-center students' penchant for reading solely for argument and a narrow conception of argument at that, I missed the opportunity to engage students in exploring the holistic ways in which we construct meaning, ways that certainly interact with the rational domain but cannot be limited to it. Students, for example, were not given the chance to explore, interpret, and articulate their emotional responses to some pretty powerfully ideological texts or to hear the responses of other readers. They were not encouraged to mobilize this epistemology as a means to engage and critique the texts.

By shifting my students' attention away from argument and to more stylistic features of texts, which I did in good faith, I continued to obscure the role emotion likely played in students' readings of these authors' texts, thereby suggesting that engaging with a text is a strictly rational enterprise. Of course, we know it is not, and Elizabeth Vogel (2009:201) has addressed the significant implications of neglecting emotion in the classroom: "This fear of emotion may hinder deep interrogation of a subject and one major consequence of this is that we never leave the prescribed 'way' of thinking and speaking about these topics. And since the topics that produce the most tension and fear in the classroom are the ones that connect to oppressed people, the oppression remains. Either our discussions fall along familiar lines or silence ensues. Both avenues allow injustice to remain and the status quo to continue." In one of the most foundational pieces on emotion in the field of rhetoric and composition, Lynn Worsham (1998:216) similarly argues: "If our commitment is to real individual and social change . . . our most urgent political and pedagogical task remains the fundamental reeducation of emotion. This project cannot succeed by mapping a new regime of meaning onto an old way of feeling, one that has only intensified with the so-called 'waning of affect' in the era of the postmodern."

Situating reading as an act of empathy in that first-year writing course may have also been a viable approach to offering students a more comprehensive and richer rhetorical context in which to read and write, one that would have forestalled students' rush to call these authors hypocrites. My conceptualization of reading as an empathic act responds to Patrick Sullivan's (2014:118) call for "a new writing curriculum built around listening, empathy, and reflection," which, as he notes, "would help nurture essential cognitive and dispositional orientations that are the wellsprings of mature meaning-making." When I describe reading as an act of empathy, I am invoking reading's social nature wherein a reader enters into a "transaction" with the text, a term Louise Rosenblatt used in the late 1930s to describe the practice of reading but that was not really recognized and popularized until the height of reader-response theory decades later. Rosenblatt's (2005:xviii–xix) choice of the word *transaction* to explain the relationship between reader and text was a deliberate one, as she explained in an interview with Nicholas Karolides:

> In 1949 John Dewey and Arthur E. Bentley suggested that the term "interaction" was too much involved with the older stimulus-and-response approach. They suggested "transaction" for the idea of a continuing to-and-fro, back and forth, give-and-take reciprocal or spiral relationship in which each conditions the other. "Transaction" has implications for all aspects of life. Ecology offers an easily-understood illustration of the transactional relationship between human beings and their natural environment. "Transaction" also applies to individuals' relations to one another, whether we think of them in the family, the classroom, the school or in the broader society and culture. This approach had been an important part of my thinking, so that I welcomed the term transaction, to emphasize that the

meaning is being built up through the back-and-forth relationship between reader and text during a reading event.

The reading I am describing here, which is based on Rosenblatt's concept of a transaction in which "meaning is being
built up through the back-and-forth relationship between
reader and text," is along the lines of what Donna Qualley
(1997:62) calls "essayistic reading" wherein "readers put themselves at risk by opening themselves to multiple and contrasting
perspectives of others [whether within or outside of the text]
while reflexively monitor[ing] their own beliefs and reactions
to the process."

To be truly empathic and a truly empathic reader, as defined
at the beginning of this chapter, though, readers would go
beyond what Qualley describes by not just opening themselves
to the perspectives of others but by identifying with and mir-
roring those perspectives as they strive to understand the text
and its ideas from within and, moreover, from a more holistic
space that invites feeling and emotion rather than just reason.
In other words, empathic reading involves mobilizing empathy
as a means to complement more rational methods of understanding. I am not suggesting that empathy is the only or even
the primary way of constructing meaning but that it is deliberately called upon to complement more rationally inflected
methods.

Empathic reading might also be thought of in terms of an
"alignment" toward a text, a term used by Robert J. Tierney and
P. David Pearson (1983:572) to describe "two facets: stances a
reader or writer assumes in collaboration with their author or
audience, and roles within which the reader or writer immerse
themselves as they proceed with the topic. In other words,"
Tierney and Pearson (1983:572) continue, "as readers and writers approach a text they vary the nature of their stance or collaboration with their author (if they are a reader) or audience
(if they are a writer) and, in conjunction with this collaboration, immerse themselves in a variety of roles." Just as I am not
suggesting that empathic reading be the sole way students are
asked to read,[14] Tierney and Pearson (1983:576) point out that

a focus on alignment "does not necessitate bridling readers and writers to one another. Indeed, we would hypothesize that new insights are more likely discovered and appreciations derived when readers and writers try out different alignments as they read and write their texts." As Tierney and Pearson suggest, thinking about alignment allows one to explore the connection between reading and writing as it applies to the rhetorical positioning of both reader and writer such that it moves us to thinking beyond the purely rational dimension.

A largely unexplored precedent for thinking beyond the rational and about the role of emotions in rhetorical education comes to us from Aristotle, as Ellen Quandahl (2003) points out. Although Aristotle and classical rhetorical education is most often represented as separating reason from emotion rather than considering the ways they complement each other, Quandahl (2003:11) argues convincingly that "Aristotle is an indispensable predecessor for acknowledging and working with rather than against emotion in rhetorical education." Quandahl points to how Aristotle situates emotions as social in nature, describes virtues as dependent on one's capacity to feel, and defines emotions as rhetorical. In so doing, she recognizes an early, albeit incomplete, way Aristotle gestures toward the need to address "how emotion might figure in a rhetorical pedagogy" (Quandahl 2003:21). Situating reading as an act of empathy offers a way of further developing this strand in Aristotle's work, as well as a potential antidote to students' rush to judgment during their reading.

In his call for less antagonistic modes of argumentation (as detailed in chapter 5), Jim W. Corder (1985) offers a useful metaphorical image that helps us imagine what empathic reading might look like, particularly in opposition to the kind of reading my students were practicing. Corder (1985:6) describes a kind of argumentation that involves an "untiring stretch toward the other, a reach toward enfolding the other." If we define reading as an empathic act in which the reader imagines the feelings of the other (e.g., the author) that inform the beliefs in texts and "stretches toward" and "moves toward enfolding that other," then one's entire orientation toward texts has changed. Those students who were reading narrowly for argument and were adamant that these authors were "hypocrites" would have necessarily produced different readings, or at least they would not have so quickly, uncritically, and unwaveringly settled on this interpretation. My goal here is not to shut down potential interpretations but rather to reflect on how expanding my own understanding of rhetorical education and using that expanded understanding to readjust the context in which I teach reading may lead to a more comprehensive and nuanced rhetorical education for my students, who are living in a climate that underscores how truly entangled reason and emotion are.

Although I noticed students' pattern of reading for argument, described above, almost as soon as I began teaching in 2001, that article was largely based on my first class during my first semester at a new institution as a newly minted PhD. One could therefore chalk my response to students' narrow ways of reading up to a rookie mistake. As satisfying as that theory would be, it's not accurate, to which the following far more recent example attests.

In 2017 I published a piece in the *English Journal* titled "How Students Read: Some Thoughts on Why This Matters" wherein, among other things, I describe the benefits of Peter Elbow's Doubting and Believing Game. I have praised this approach in other venues, including in this very book. Elbow's exercise or "game," as he calls it, involves inhabiting multiple perspectives (i.e., believing and doubting). Elbow (2008:170–71) explains that this "continual practice in trying to have other perceptions and experiences helps people break out of their 'sets' and preoccupations—helps them be less rigid, less prey to conventional, knee-jerk, or idiosyncratic responses." Such an exercise is especially important in today's divisive climate, particularly when we consider the emphasis Elbow places on listening and silence in the "believing" part of that game. In that essay I describe how the game can benefit students like those I mention in the much earlier *Rhetoric Review* article who "need practice believing" (Carillo 2017a:36), in part so they can recognize that there "is a difference between complexity and contradiction." In the more recent essay I note that "if students are encouraged to take the time to slow down and believe, then they will have the opportunity to explore the complexities of such varied works, as well as *how* and *why*, in some cases, these writers are using contradiction as a rhetorical device" (Carillo 2017a:36, emphasis in original). I continue, "Whether a student needs more practice doubting or believing, this way of reading helps students determine what they really think about a subject rather than what they assume they think or what they believe they should think" (Carillo 2017a:36).

Notice how in the above excerpts I assume that beliefs are strictly cognitive in nature—so much so, I may add, that I repeat the word *think* three times. Moreover, I assume that it is (only) through the rational dimension that one navigates complexity. As I return to this article, written not that long ago, I wonder what it would mean to situate the believing game, or methodological believing, as Elbow also calls it, in the emotional dimension, even though Elbow does not overtly or consistently do so himself.[15] Elbow (2008:7) largely defines "doubting" and "believing" as belonging to the rational dimension, as "tools . . . to help us think better." Describing the uses of these tools, Elbow (2008:7, emphasis added) writes:

> We need the believing game in order to achieve goals that the doubting game neglects. The believing game develops a different kind of thinking, a different dimension of our intelligence or rationality, and also a different way of *interacting with others*. This is no argument against the doubting game in itself, since it obviously develops an indispensable dimension of intelligence or rationality. The only thing I'm arguing against is the monopoly of the doubting game in our culture's notion of rationality or careful thinking—a monopoly that has led us to neglect a different and equally indispensable kind of careful thinking.

I have emphasized the phrase "interacting with others" above to underscore the social dimension of the believing game, as well as the related potential empathic nature of believing, which Elbow (2005:392) develops further: "We don't get the benefits of the believing game unless we make an active effort to believe various positions, enter into them, dwell in them; merely listening carefully or refraining from arguing with unwelcome ideas is not enough."

Although the term *belief* does not immediately suggest a relationship to emotion and largely falls into the rational domain, methodological believing, as Elbow (2008:7) describes it, also helps us "develop a different kind of thinking, a different dimension of our intelligence or rationality," since "the believing game teaches us to try to understand points of view from the inside." Elbow (2008:8) explains that "sometimes you can't understand something till you try it or act on it. This is where role playing gets its power: understanding through doing and inhabiting—not debating." Elbow's descriptions conjure up the concept of empathy as he describes believing as dwelling in positions, understanding points of view from the inside, and understanding through doing and inhabiting. Yet in my recently published article and, more important, in my pedagogy, I ignore this aspect of believing when I ask my students to participate in the believing game. Instead, I privilege its place in the rational domain. Reflecting on my limited way of understanding how Elbow is using the term *belief,* I want to imagine the value of presenting belief in the Doubting and Believing Game (and, more generally, as I do above) as having one foot in the rational and one in the emotional dimension. How might contextualizing the activity in this way change its outcomes?

It seems to me that such an approach wherein belief is akin to empathy would allow students to explore the role of emotions in making meaning and therefore in developing beliefs. Within this context, when students engage in the Doubting and Believing Game, they might be prompted to acknowledge how their emotions impact their beliefs, thereby expanding the narrower and popular, although not scientific, understanding of beliefs as residing in the cognitive realm and informed only by rationality. In so doing, the Doubting and Believing Game gives instructors and students an opportunity to think about the relationship between the rational and emotional, as well as an opportunity to help students reflect on the role of emotions in constructing meaning as they learn more sophisticated ways of reading and writing. "With regard to learning," explains Elbow (2008:8), "the doubting game teaches us to extricate or detach ourselves from ideas. In contrast, the believing game teaches us to enter into ideas—to invest or insert ourselves." What Elbow outlines here could be described as a form of empathic reading, reading that involves an "untiring stretch toward the other, a reach toward enfolding the other" (Corder 1985:26), such as an author. In other words, this exercise helps students "to enter into texts that feel "alien" to them—to dwell in them and experience them—not just criticize them" (Elbow 2008:9). The Doubting and Believing Game, then, becomes a way to invite emotion into the classroom and create a space to reflect on how emotion informs beliefs, an invitation that unfortunately escaped me as I explored only the rational aspect of the Doubting and Believing Game in my own pedagogy and scholarship.

In the interest of having enough room to explore how the field of composition and rhetoric might also address the role of empathy in its research practices, I must stop with these two examples. Still, I hope they are instructive in that they reveal my own (inadvertent) privileging of the rational and suggest ways other instructors might reveal the values embedded in their own pedagogies. If one is committed to creating a space in the classroom for exploring the role of emotion in the construction of meaning and knowledge, then revisiting one's pedagogy to make visible precisely how encumbered it may be by an emphasis on the rational at the expense of the emotional is one place to start.

EMPATHIC RESEARCH IN RHETORIC AND COMPOSITION

Thus far, this chapter has tried to demonstrate the importance of reexamining our own teaching practices to expose and address the assumptions they make about the place of emotion in the construction of meaning and knowledge. This section develops and extends a passing comment Susan McLeod (1997) makes in *Notes on the Heart: Affective Issues in the Writing Classroom* that got me thinking not about teaching practices but about research practices, and specifically, what it would mean to acknowledge the place of what I call "empathic research" in our discipline's history, as well as to call for deliberately empathic research in rhetoric and composition. McLeod (1997:114) makes the following comment, almost in passing: "It was empathy that allowed Mina Shaughnessy to look at the error-filled pages of open-admissions writers and see the logic behind the errors, to understand the 'incipient excellence.'" I have read Shaughnessy's book, as well as many pieces (both laudatory and critical) about it. Yet prior to reading McLeod's quick gloss of it (which appears at the end of a paragraph and never gets developed further), I had never thought about Shaughnessy's research in that way. Reading McLeod's perspective, though, has me thinking about how other research in our field is inflected by empathy.

This section offers a review of some of that research and imagines what it would mean to consciously incorporate attention to empathy as a form of constructing meaning, as a way of "reading" one's data particularly with participant-based research within the field of rhetoric and composition. This chapter aims to demonstrate how acknowledging the place of emotion, of empathy, in some of the most significant studies in the field demonstrates that such a focus need not be in opposition to or foreclose other methods, including the field's current commitment to more empirically based as well as replicable, aggregable, and data-supported (RAD) methods. Instead, a focus on the role of empathy in research has the potential to complement those methods in its more holistic approach to how knowledge is constructed.

First, let's start with McLeod's observation about Shaughnessy's work and parse it a bit since she does not. McLeod (1997:114) notes that "it was empathy that allowed Mina Shaughnessy to look at the error-filled pages of open-admissions writers and see the logic behind the errors, to understand . . . " McLeod observes that rather than starting from her own position, whether that of researcher or teacher (or any other position), Shaughnessy instead sought to understand error from the perspective of the students who were making the errors. Only by coming at the research from that particular angle, suggests McLeod, was Shaughnessy able to understand the *logic* of those errors, which is, of course, one of the major contributions of that book. Shaughnessy accesses the "logic" of students' errors and "understands" them not only through rational means but also through emotional means, through empathy. Certainly, I don't mean to suggest—and I don't think McLeod does either—that empathy alone is responsible for the findings in that study but rather that it is important to foreground that epistemology and what it brings to research in the form of a "more inclusive knowledge-making process" (Royster 2000:254).

I would posit that the research on error following *Errors and Expectations*, which *Errors and Expectations* made possible, could also be said to emerge from empathy, from a commitment to reading the problem at hand—in this case "error"—from the perspective of the one making the errors rather than some supposedly objective position (Shaughnessey 1979). We see this in David Bartholomae's (2016:21) Braddock Award Winning essay "The Study of Error," wherein he argues that to better understand the errors "that emerge when beginning writers are faced with complex tasks," research must be conducted using the method of "error analysis." This method is based on a theory of errors that imagines them as "necessary stages of individual development" and "data that provide insight into the idiosyncratic strategies of a particular language user at a particular point in his acquisition of a target language" (Bartholomae 2016:22). The theory of error that guides Bartholomae's research is empathic in its investment in getting inside the student writer's mind to identify the source of the error rather than to simply mark it as such. This work enables the instructor to "plan instruction to assist a writer's *internal* syllabus" rather than "impose an inappropriate or even misleading syllabus on a learner" (Bartholomae 2016:24, emphasis added). What Bartholomae describes as a writer's "internal syllabus" shifts attention to students' internal processes as opposed to what Jane Tompkins (1996:221) calls an "externally oriented" curriculum that deals with "externalized bodies of knowledge."

To ask why students make the errors they do is to take a more holistic approach to a research problem, one that creates a space to consider those internal processes. To take on the role of error-analyst, then, as do Bartholomae and Richard Haswell, discussed below, does not involve distancing oneself from the learner but constitutes an "untiring stretch toward" the student to better "read" a learner's needs from the inside rather than imposing those needs from the outside.

Like Bartholomae, Haswell (1988) takes up error analysis in "Error and Change in College Student Writing," and he also does so as an empathic reader of data. Haswell's study of error in college students' writing is situated as a direct response to— if not corrective of—Albert R. Kitzhaber's (1963) famous study of Dartmouth students' writing. Whereas Kitzhaber's findings indicate that Dartmouth seniors make more surface errors in their writing than do first-year students, Haswell probes the specific errors students make. This allows him to conclude that what Kitzhaber characterizes as nothing more than an increase in error is actually a "liability" of the "push toward other kinds of syntactic complexity, especially toward modification of nominals and greater sentence size" (Haswell 1988:489). Whereas Kitzhaber's approach to errors—namely, counting them—suggests the Western world's "affinity for the rational and the scientific [that] has left little room for anything that cannot be observed, counted, or measured" (Richmond 2002:71), Haswell (1988:481) contextualizes the errors he notices in students' writing by "reading" them in terms of growth, a perspective he largely borrows from educational and cognitive psychology, which he describes as follows: "Inner human maturation is hypothesized not as a simple sequence of discreet stages, but as an ongoing multidimensional interaction where the temporary mastery of one skill may impede the learning of another." In describing the multidimensional nature of maturation and growth, which in its "multidimensionality" presumably also includes an emotional dimension, Haswell takes a more holistic approach to error than does Kitzhaber, which allows him, like Shaughnessy, to read the errors from the students' perspectives.

Despite what we might call the empathic undertones of the studies described above, Bartholomae and Haswell employ a range of methods in their research, including empirical methods, case studies, reading-aloud protocols, one-on-one interviews, and both qualitative and quantitative analyses. This is important because the kind of empathic research I will call for at the end of this chapter should be understood as complementary to these approaches and not in opposition to them.

Around the same time Bartholomae and Haswell were exploring ways of understanding student error so the expanding population of college students could be better served, Glynda Hull and Mike Rose were interested in related questions surrounding remediation, research that I also think is inflected by empathy. I would argue that their methods of studying students' "unconventional" readings in their Braddock Award Winning essay " 'This Wooden Shack Place': The Logic of an Unconventional Reading" are infused by empathy in ways that are even more apparent than in Bartholomae's and Haswell's studies, precisely because Hull and Rose (1990) take emotion into consideration as they strive to understand why Robert, the student discussed in their piece, reads the way he does. In the exchanges they analyze, Robert is discussing a poem titled "And Your Soul Shall Dance" by Japanese American writer Garrett Kaoru Hongo, the focus of a class session taught by Mike Rose. In trying to understand Robert's "perception of the shacks," a key symbol in the poem, Hull and Rose (1990:278) explain that

> Robert's background makes it unlikely that he is going to respond to "a small cluster of wooden shacks" in quite the same way—with quite the same emotional reaction—as would a conventional (and most likely middle-class) reader for whom the shacks might function as a quickly discernable, emblematic literary device. Some of Robert's relatives in Trinidad still live in houses like those described in the poem, and his early housing in Los Angeles . . . was quite modest . . . this might make certain images less foreign to him, and, therefore, less emotionally striking . . . might not spark the same dramatic response in him as in a conventional/middle-class reader.

Notice how Hull and Rose recognize the way Robert's emotions impact how he (mis)reads an "emblematic literary device." They are not inclined to mark this "error" with red pen but to "read" it from the inside. But Hull and Rose cannot know for sure what Robert is feeling and the extent to which the familial experiences described in the above excerpt impact the way he composes meaning. Instead, they must imagine his feelings. As the definitions of empathy at the beginning of this chapter indicate, empathy does not necessarily involve the observation of an emotion in someone else but includes imagining that emotion. It is by imagining how Robert feels and feeling like him that Hull and Rose are able to recognize why he reads the poem as he does. The poem simply does not affect him emotionally the same way it would affect other readers for whom the image of a shack has different emotional associations. In this particular example, not only do the researchers observe and comment on the degree to which Robert's emotions allowed him to assign value to the image of the shack, but an emotion—namely, empathy—seemingly enables the researchers themselves to more holistically understand Robert's reading practices.

In one of Hull and Rose's later essays, "Rethinking Remediation: Toward a Social-Cognitive Understanding of Problematic Reading and Writing," which laid the groundwork for Rebecca Moore Howard's theories about patchwriting, discussed below, Hull and Rose (1989) follow Tanya, a nineteen-year-old student in a community college. They conduct formal interviews, hold informal discussions with her, and review her essays over the course of a semester to better understand what happens "when the student sits down to write" (Hull and Rose 1989:143). In the instance analyzed in their essay, Tanya has been asked to summarize a sample case study written by a nurse, since Tanya indicated interest in becoming a nurse herself. The summary Tanya writes is largely copied from the case study, pieces of it totally lifted with others semi-lifted, all patched together. Most striking, though, about Tanya's story is the way Hull and Rose construct it, how they develop their understanding of Tanya's "plagiarism." They do so through identification, through empathy, explaining, "We forget that we, like Tanya, continually appropriate each other's language to establish group membership, to grow, and to define ourselves in new ways, and that such appropriation is a fundamental part of language use, even as the appearance of our texts belies it" (Hull and Rose 1989:152). Seeing themselves in Tanya, Hull and Rose's conclusions about why Tanya "plagiarizes" are based on their empathic reading of Tanya's situation, of their kinship with Tanya and her writing practices.

In Rebecca Moore Howard's research that draws on Hull and Rose's study of Tanya, Howard (1992:235) is looking for a way to understand "why one-third of a class of students in a prestigious liberal arts college—the CEOs of tomorrow—had blandly stumbled into plagiarism." She explores various definitions of plagiarism and of summary writing, and she examines her own assumptions about plagiarism. But it was when Howard (1992:239) saw in her students' difficulties her own difficulties as an academic that she began to understand what was happening: "If we faculty have difficulty comprehending and manipulating the languages of the various academic cultures, how much more difficult a task do undergraduates face as they are presented with a bewildering array of discourse[,] none of which resonates with the languages of their homes or secondary schools." In effect, the concept of patchwriting emerged from an act of identification, from Howard's empathy for her students. The role of empathy in such work is particularly significant when one considers that the concept of patchwriting informs how "plagiarism" is currently understood and addressed in colleges and universities across the country, as well as that Rebecca Moore Howard was asked to weigh in on the recently appointed US Supreme Court Justice Neil Gorsuch's own brush with plagiarism.

The final example of what I am calling empathic research comes from researcher Jacqueline Jones Royster (2000) who, unlike the researchers whose work I have reviewed above, is forthright about the role her emotions played in the study of the literacy practices of well-educated nineteenth-century African

American women she details in *Traces of a Stream: Literacy and Social Change among African American Women.* Patricia Bizzell (2000:13) describes Royster's (2000) unapologetic identification with the subjects of her study: "She articulates an approach that frankly begins in her identification . . . with the subjects of her inquiries . . . On the one hand, this is a deeply personal identification, springing from a mutual African American heritage . . . and she shares her story of community allegiances and multiple experiences with extant archives on African American women, with colleagues on the scholarly journal *SAGE,* and with her students at Spelman College. At the same time, Royster pointedly rejects an essentialized notion of identity." Working overtly within feminist research methods that reject objectivity as the gold standard (or even desirable or attainable), Royster foregrounds the emotional connections that not only inform her research but that shape and guide it and, in this case, constitute its source. In fact, *Traces of a Stream* is far more than a study of literacy practices; it is an exercise in empathic reading, what Royster (2000:254, 277) describes as a "more inclusive knowledge-making process" that "maximiz[es] the interpretive power of various standpoints by bringing all that we know together kaleidoscopically." Yet Royster's empathy it is not uncritical or unreflective, for as Bizzell notes above, although Royster identifies with her subjects, she simultaneously rejects an essentialized notion of identity.

Bizzell's point that Royster avoids essentializing identity despite her identification with her subjects suggests one of the potential liabilities of empathy and the sort of empathic research I am reviewing and will call for in the conclusion to this chapter. In empathizing with another, including research subjects, one runs the risk of erasing that other altogether. Jonathan Alexander and Jacqueline Rhodes (2014:431) call this a "flattening effect," as "the 'other' is tamed as a knowable entity." Amy Shuman (2005:5) describes further implications of uncritical empathy: "Empathy offers the possibility of understanding across space and time, but it rarely changes the circumstances of those who suffer." In *Scenes of Subjection: Terror, Slavery, and Self-Making in Nineteenth-Century America,* dedicated to exploring how black identities were shaped during and in the aftermath of slavery, Saidiya Hartman (1997:19) writes, "Empathy is double-edged, for in making the other's suffering one's own, this suffering is occluded by the other's obliteration." Thus, as I move to the conclusion of this chapter, I want to emphasize that I am not advocating that researchers employ empathic reading practices of their data that are driven by uncritical empathy but rather a practice that resembles more closely what Todd DeStigter (1999:240), drawing on Jay Robinson's definition of "critical empathy," describes as follows: "The process of establishing informed and affective connections with other human beings, of thinking and feeling with them at some emotionally, intellectually, and socially significant level, while always remembering that such connections are complicated by sociohistorical forces that hinder the equitable, just relationships that we presumably seek." In the following section I bring together the two strands of this chapter to detail further what this conception of critical empathy offers our teaching of critical reading as well as our research.

CONCLUDING THOUGHTS

In this chapter I have described a two-pronged approach to making empathy more central in the field of rhetoric and composition, namely, through our teaching and research practices. I have maintained the importance of considering how our current pedagogies are likely informed by a bias against affect and emotion, and I have offered detailed accounts of how I imagine revising the ways I have previously gone about expanding students' meaning-making practices. I have also posited that some of the most significant research in the field of rhetoric and composition is inflected by empathy (to differing degrees, of course). By way of conclusion, I want to lay out what all this might mean for the field of rhetoric and composition generally as well as specifically within our particularly divisive climate.

Incorporating attention to empathy in our teaching and research supports the field's current focus on dispositions, habits of mind, "meaningful writing projects," and generally more

holistic ways of thinking about learning and assessing that learning, particularly (although not exclusively) at the postsecondary level.[16] For example, the *Framework for Success in Postsecondary
Writing* (2011), as mentioned in chapter 2, lists eight habits of
mind "essential for success in college writing." The Association
of American Colleges and Universities' (AACU) report titled
"College Learning for the New Global Century" (2007), as
well as its fifteen "VALUE rubrics" (AACU 2009a, 2009b) that
address everything from civic engagement to creative thinking,
do not just emphasize intellectual competencies but also value
other aspects of learning, including risk taking, which "may
include personal risk (fear of embarrassment or rejection)";
"communication strategies," such as listening; and the ability
to adjust one's own "attitudes and beliefs because of working
within and learning from [a] diversity of communities and cultures" (AACU 2009a, 2009b). Recent work on the transfer of
learning has also shifted its focus toward students' dispositions
(Driscoll and Wells 2012). Beyond the ways a focus on critical
empathy can support current frameworks in the field, a focus
on critical empathy can also go a long way toward enriching and
expanding those frameworks.

   Although this chapter addresses both the pedagogical and
research-oriented implications of making empathy a more consciously central feature of our work, a significant portion of the
scholarship on emotion and empathy that has been published
in the field of rhetoric and composition since the affective turn
has considered empathy largely as a pedagogical tool, a way to
ground students' practice in taking on different perspectives
and incorporating counterarguments into their writing. Some
scholars such as Eric Leake (2016) and Robert Scholes (2002)
have detailed how empathy can be explored through reading
texts that simultaneously "invite and frustrate identification"
(Leake 2016). Empathy has also been mobilized in classrooms
as a means of rhetorical analysis that allows students to recognize how "images, music, and advertisements use empathy to
foster identification" (Leake 2016). All of these approaches
offer productive methods of incorporating empathy into the

classroom, but none of them goes as far as this chapter does in arguing for a more comprehensive focus on empathy that would inform not just our teaching but also our research.

Even when scholarship from the affective turn and from the recent special issue of *Composition Forum* (summer 2016) looks at the role of emotion beyond the classroom setting, it stops short of addressing composition *research* as a potential site in which to foreground in more explicit ways (or perhaps more explicitly rhetorical terms) what emotions do, how they are bound up with how we make meaning, and how emotions and reason are interconnected. Surely, there have been important contributions surrounding the place of emotion in writing program administration (WPA) scholarship, most notably Diana George's (1999) *Kitchen Cooks, Plate Twirlers, and Troubadours: Writing Program Administrators Tell Their Stories* and Micciche's (2002) "More Than a Feeling," in which she describes WPA work in terms of disappointment. In addition to disappointment, Richard Miller (1999) and Mara Holt (1999) have explored the fear and loneliness associated with WPA work. Despite the range of scholarship on emotion that emerged during the affective turn and since, as well as the increasingly privileged position of dispositions and habits of mind in our field, research practices somehow remain off the table, as if they are somehow immune to emotion. There are, of course, any number of reasons for this. For decades, the field of rhetoric and composition has resisted its marginalized status, its position as the "stepchild" of literary studies. Scholars have called for moving beyond the anecdotal (Salvatori 2002) in our research, for more empirically based studies (Charney 1996), and for RAD research (Haswell 2005). The field's professional organizations have introduced awards to honor this type of work and grants and fellowships to fund it. To foreground emotion in our work might seem to some a move in the wrong direction. I remind you, though, that all of the studies reviewed in this chapter use a range of methodologies that are not undermined by the role empathy also plays in their research. Moreover, as the scientific studies glossed in the beginning of this chapter indicate, cognitive psychology has come to accept the interdependence of emotion and cognition.

Perhaps one of the most common objections to "inserting" emotion (as if it is otherwise absent) into one's research is that emotion gets in the way of the researcher's objectivity. Emotion has long been associated with bias, with distorting reason and otherwise objective perceptions and understandings, a point that is picked up in chapter 5. Emotions like identification and empathy are especially "dangerous" in this way if one's goal is to access how other people behave, think, read, and write and even how they transfer all of this from one context to another. Yet as historical antecedents of the work I am calling for, the impactful—if not groundbreaking—studies I review in this chapter indicate the potential in research that is characterized by the empathic reading of one's data. In these studies, empathy is enabling and productive and does not eclipse or undermine the research at hand. In fact, reading their data empathically allows researchers to observe, listen, and make meaning from the perspectives of study participants. Moreover, it is largely through this reading practice, this act of identification, that some of their most significant findings emerge.

It should be clear by now that what I am calling empathic research does not mean studying or researching emotion, the same way empathic reading pedagogies don't necessarily involve teaching students about emotion. Instead, empathic research is research that is not afraid of recognizing in our research the range of ways we construct meaning and knowledge. Taken to its extreme, conducting empathic research might mean setting a research agenda that deliberately allows for these emotionally inflected ways of knowing when conducting participant-based studies. In the end, we need to become more comfortable with recognizing the range of ways everyone, including researchers, composes meaning. Foregrounding empathy as one of many ways of composing meaning and constructing knowledge need not—and should not—be simply about celebrating this emotion but a means to think critically about it, to explore how it complicates and enriches our work.

As Peter Elbow (2003:vii) observes in his foreword to *A Way to Move*, "When we ignore emotions and go only for logical thinking, we are liable to miss crucial things—not just in us but in the world." What if Shaughnessy had read those mistakes as nothing more than errors in need of correction? Or Hull and Rose hadn't identified with Tanya's struggle? Or Howard didn't recognize in one-third of her students the same difficulties she encountered as an academic? Their research, nay, composition and rhetoric as a field, would look very different today.

As we encourage our students, particularly in this divisive climate, to tap into their belief systems by exploring the role emotion plays in these systems, we might also consider the importance of this work to democracy. Thomas Jefferson and John Dewey after him believed that to function as it should, democracy needs an educated citizenry. In light of what we know about the relationship between cognition and emotion, we need to expand our reading pedagogies to include attention to our students' emotions so that the citizenry is educated in a more holistic manner. "A democratic society . . . needs citizens with the imagination to see what political doctrines mean for human beings," writes Louise Rosenblatt (1983:184–86), which can be achieved by helping our students "develop the capacity to feel intensely the needs and sufferings and aspirations of people whose personal interests are distinct from our own, people with whom we may have no bond other than our common humanity." Rosenblatt is describing the cultivation of empathy. The classroom can support this work by creating a space in which students "listen with understanding to what others have to say and . . . respond in relevant terms" (Rosenblatt 1983:71). I think we would be wise to do the same in our research—to capitalize on the generative relationship between "our emotional constitution" and "our theorizing," which Alison Jaggar (1989:147) describes as a "continuous feedback loop" "such that each continually modifies the other and is in principle inseparable from it." To do so would be to recognize the largely unexamined emotional dimension of our research while partaking in and continuing the tradition of empathic research important to our field's history.

4

MODELING READING
THROUGH ANNOTATION

On January 20, 2017, *Time* magazine published a piece titled "Trump, Annotated" on its online site. It was one of hundreds, maybe thousands, of articles published about Trump's inaugural address. As its title suggests, this particular piece isn't just about Trump's speech but is a transcript of that speech that has been annotated—in this case by former president George H.W. Bush's speechwriter Elise Jordan. Other, similar pieces with fully annotated transcripts of Trump's inaugural address were published in periodicals, on websites, and on social-media platforms, including the *New York Times*, the *Washington Post*, NPR, and Vox.com. Trump is not the first president to have his speeches annotated. In fact, it was a move made by the Obama administration in 2015 that forced journalism's hand, as Benjamin Mullin (2016), managing editor of Poynter.org, noted: "President Obama broke with a longtime White House tradition by leapfrogging the press for his annual State of the Union Speech. Rather than circulating not-for-publication copies of his remarks to reporters in advance, as had been custom, the Obama camp published them on *Medium* for everyone to read." By publishing a full transcript of a president's speech, the White House removed the cachet reserved for the periodicals that managed to get access. The *Washington Post* and other media outlets had to find a way to remain relevant, and if it wasn't through publishing per se, it would be through the commentary—in the form of annotations—they provided alongside the published primary source documents.

In 2015 Chris Cillizza, lead writer of the *Washington Post*'s politics blog *The Fix*, claimed that "annotation is the future of

DOI: 10.7330/9781607327912.c004

journalism" because it "hold[s] almost limitless potential as an avenue by which journalists can add value." In 2016, amid the tumultuous presidential campaign, Cillizza (personal email to Poynter.org, August 2016) stood by his claim, reiterating that annotation offers an "enhanced reader experienc[e] that journalism can and should move toward." Cillizza believes people are "looking for context and commentary with their news" and that journalists are in a unique position to provide both. While this may, in fact, be a watershed moment for journalism, this chapter contends that it is also a watershed moment for reading. Often represented as a silent, solitary act, this shift in journalistic practices has put reading front and center, drawing attention to its social dimension. These annotated documents—these representations of reading as an active, complex process—become particularly important when thought of in the context of a post-truth culture that to really prosper depends on the passivity of its citizens. These annotated documents also serve as a foil to the oversimplified and, frankly, inaccurate description of reading presented by the Common Core State Standards (CCSS), as discussed in chapter 2.

Writing instructors could take a lesson from what annotation has meant for journalism. Annotating primary source documents has allowed journalists to concretize the reading process, to make visible an otherwise invisible process, and to theorize and demonstrate the role context and commentary play in strong reading. Through the circulation of these annotated documents, many of which are available online and get annotated by several readers through platforms like Genius, journalists have made reading a collaborative enterprise that goes far beyond the relationship between a single reader and the text. Through this "community approach," which "forwards the idea of a reporter as a first-among-equals in leading an ongoing and evolving effort to understand a topic" (Cillizza 2015), journalists and others who contribute to the annotation of these public documents are modeling what it means to be in dialogue not just with a text but with other readers about that text, to invest in providing the "context and commentary" necessary to make that text accessible, and to make it all around more comprehensive.

This chapter contends that making annotation central to the teaching of reading and writing at the postsecondary level can have a similarly powerful impact on literacy pedagogies. I'm arguing here for teaching—not just expecting—students to annotate. I'm arguing for making annotation the central practice, the primary tool instructors use to teach the connected practices of reading and writing. I'm arguing for using annotation to foreground the often-neglected social dimension of reading. As long as reading remains invisible, we cannot work on reading in the classroom as easily as we work on writing. If we can't work on reading, how can we help our students become informed, engaged citizens in a democracy that depends on their participation? We can't. As such, this chapter explores the untapped potential of annotation as a tool that can be used to directly address and teach critical reading in the classroom. Although it is not *the* solution to the difficulties students face with reading (see chapter 2 for qualitative and quantitative evidence of these difficulties), foregrounding annotation to help students imagine ways of engaging, evaluating, and responding to texts is a strategic, targeted rejoinder to the current climate. Specifically, a pedagogy that puts annotation front and center allows instructors to

- Concretize and explore the social nature of reading
- Connect the practices of reading and writing so students develop their abilities in both simultaneously
- Directly teach ways of reading that prepare students to function in a post-truth culture
- Explore productive and "expert" ways of reading through models of annotation.

This chapter assumes that the practice of annotation is taught within a mindful reading framework, a concept I have explored in *Securing a Place for Reading in Composition: The Importance of Teaching for Transfer* (Carillo 2015) and elsewhere. The mindful reading framework is not another type of reading that might appear on a list alongside rhetorical reading, for example, but a framework that contains the range of reading strategies students might be taught, such as annotation, the Doubting and Believing Game, and Reading Like a Writer (popularized by Mike Bunn). Within this framework, instructors choose, define, and teach the reading strategies they imagine will be most useful to students and give students regular opportunities to reflect on their reading practices while positioning them to transfer these practices to other courses and contexts.

I use the term *mindful* to underscore the meta-cognitive basis of this frame wherein students become knowledgeable, deliberate, and reflective about how they read and what different reading approaches allow and enable. Mindful reading is related to "mindfulness," a concept often associated with Buddhism and used frequently in the field of psychology. The term *mindful,* when modifying reading, describes a particular stance on the part of the reader, one that is open, flexible, and characterized by intentional awareness of and attention to the present moment and the demands it makes on reading. This intense awareness—the key to transfer—helps student-readers construct knowledge about reading and about themselves as readers. As this chapter explores, annotation becomes a powerful tool for addressing reading, as it allows instructors to capitalize on annotation's capacity to make the elusive practice of reading visible to students and instructors.

MAKING READING VISIBLE

Although writing gets a great deal of attention across the disciplines, reading does not (Horning 2007). Robert Scholes (2002:166) blames reading's invisibility: "We accept [that writing must continue to be taught in college] . . . because we can see writing, and we know that much of the writing we see is not good enough. But we do not see reading . . . I am certain, though, that if we could see it, we would be appalled." Unlike students' writing, which we collect and provide feedback on or distribute to other students to provide feedback on in peer tutoring sessions, we can't do the same with reading. To address reading as consistently as we address writing, we must make it visible.

Requiring students to annotate while they read is one way of making reading visible so that it can be worked on in the classroom. I have found that students often prefer highlighting to annotation, which may serve them well in classes where the only goal is recall but will not be as productive when instructors expect students to engage with the reading on a deeper level. Although students may bring with them some experience with annotation, they don't know much about it, how to use it productively, when to annotate, or what to annotate. Mary Goldschmidt (2010) has developed what she calls "a meta-reading checklist," inserted below, to guide students' annotations. This list, which has been a great resource for me as an instructor, gives students a wide range of options for interacting with each text they encounter. These are options students often don't imagine on their own but that help them engage in the sort of critical work we expect of them. Moreover, making these options visible to students lays the critical foundation they need to write productively about the texts they read.

GOLDSCHMIDT'S META-READING CHECKLIST

Examine each of your marginal notes and identify what function it is performing.

<u>Does it identify</u>:

- the main argument/thesis
- a new point
- an example
- evidence being used to support a point or sub-point
- why the passage is important
- a contradiction

<u>Does it comment on</u> (praise/criticize/question, agree/disagree with, or otherwise evaluate):

- the author's idea(s)

- the author's logic, examples, evidence
- the author's analysis
- the author's assumptions
- the author's methodology

Does it:

- offer an alternative explanation
- offer additional or contradictory evidence
- pose new questions
- react emotionally to the author's style, tone, or substance[?]
- make a connection with your extra-textual knowledge (or experience)

Does it in some way comment on or examine:

- how the author attends to, or fails to attend to, readers' needs (for data, for acknowledgment of differing perspectives, etc.)
- the effectiveness of how the author responds to other scholars in the field
- the scope of the author's knowledge of the debate that he/she has entered
- the author's mastery of relevant scholarship
- how the author establishes or undermines his/her own credibility
- the author's implied political stance and/or ideological grounding. (Goldschmidt 2010, 65)

Goldschmidt's meta-reading checklist provides a way for students to become aware of their own reading practices. I ask students to notice which kinds of commentary they tend to include in the margins of their texts. Do they spend most of their time marking the piece's arguments and evidence? Is their commentary evaluative? Is their commentary more personal in nature? As students become more aware of how they read, they can then develop reading goals that allow them to focus on enriching their ways of reading. They can track how well they are progressing toward their individual reading goals by tracking their annotations throughout the semester. It doesn't take long for students to realize that they need to adjust how they read (and annotate) depending on the related writing assignment.

Because these marginal notes represent the initial ways students are participating in a conversation with the author of the text, they must be undertaken purposefully so that students can develop them later as they complete the formal writing assignments for the course.

HELPING STUDENTS "IMAGINE A WORKING MODEL OF THE READER"

As important as it is for students to develop an understanding of their reading practices so they can enrich their repertoires as necessary, many students are unable to even "imagine a working model of the reader" (Bartholomae and Petrosky 1986:17). Throughout their years in school, students have picked up on the unfortunate reality that reading—like most academic subjects—is defined by the educational system in terms of mastery: you either get it right or wrong. This approach to reading is certainly represented in the Common Core State Standards, as discussed in chapter 2. Educational psychologists David N. Perkins and Gavriel Salomon (2012:256) explain this phenomenon: "For many teachers and students, knowledge of whatever sort is something to 'possess,' to have in the mental warehouse ready for deployment as required. The key question for these teachers and their students becomes whether students can show knowledge on demand—through assignments and tests that relatively directly call for what hopefully has been learned." They call this familiar conception of education "a learning culture of demand," and while they don't deny its uses, which include preparing students for high-stakes standardized exams, they take issue with its exercises and tests, which are "direct rather than open-ended," and its "courses and units," which tend to be "encapsulated rather than richly cross-connected" (Perkins and Salomon 2012:257).

We see some evidence of how this conception of education informs reading instruction through our own students' ideas about reading, such as their unattainable (and undesirable) obsession with remembering every bit of a text—sometimes perpetuated by standardized, multiple-choice–driven testing and similar assessments in the classroom—and their "concern for getting the right meaning" (Bartholomae and Petrosky 1986:17). This attitude toward reading "puts our students in an impossible position," write Bartholomae and Petrosky (1986:17). "The very gap between a text and a reader's version of a text, the gap that makes reading possible, stands for our students as a sign that they cannot read" (Bartholomae and Petrosky 1986:17).[17] And so, students need models of what it looks like to read, to do this work, to compose their versions of the text. As Bartholomae and Petrosky (1986:18) explain, "They need to learn, in other words, to create the kind of index that a more experienced reader creates by putting checks in the margin or circling page numbers or in some way indicating sections or phrases that seem interesting or puzzling or significant, sections or phrases they can turn to later when they need to work up an account of what they've read." Even in Billy Collins's (1996:17–22) poem "Marginalia," the "student method" of annotating is represented as impoverished: "Students are more modest / needing to leave only their splayed footprints / along the shore of the page. / One scrawls 'Metaphor' next to a stanza of Eliot's. / Another notes the presence of 'Irony' / 50 times outside the paragraphs of *A Modest Proposal.*" Students need models of what to look for in texts and how to respond to those texts, how to be engaged readers within an academic context lest their response to a text consists of a single word repeated fifty times in the margin.

Because annotation concretizes the act of reading, it can also be used to model the work readers do so students can begin to imagine models of reading that are not dependent on total recall and "getting the right meaning." The use of models in the field of composition is controversial, to say the least, as evidenced by the debates about the value of the templates Gerald Graff and Cathy Birkenstein (2015) include in the handbook *They Say/I Say.* Besides very narrowly focused responses to Graff and Birkenstein's approach, modeling and imitation exercises have not been all that openly or consistently discussed in the field of composition in decades—not since the demise of formalist pedagogies in the late 1970s, which also meant the demise of modeling and imitative exercises considered too prescriptive and impediments to students' creativity and individuality. In "Apologies and Accommodations: Imitation and the Writing Process," Frank Farmer and Phillip Arrington (1993) declare that one of the greatest losses associated with the fall of formalism is the subsequent rejection of imitation as a viable and theoretically sound pedagogical approach to writing instruction. According to Farmer and Arrington (1993:71), imitation exercises wherein students mimic the formal characteristics of model sentences or paragraphs have fallen into disrepute because of "attitudes inherited from our not too distant Romantic past." Following up on Farmer and Arrington's survey of scholarship on imitation since the 1960s and their argument that scholars consistently felt the need to justify their use of imitation by connecting it to process pedagogies, Robert Connors (2000) points out in "The Erasure of the Sentence" that articles on imitation (along with sentence combining and related exercises) practically disappeared by 1995. With the exception of Paul Butler (2008) and some others who drew the field's attention to stylistic studies a few years ago, scholarship in composition and rhetoric has not addressed the uses of imitative exercises in decades.

COMPLICATING "COMPOSITION'S OFFICIAL LINE"

Despite "composition's official line" that "imitation is incompatible with process approaches to the teaching of writing" (Farmer and Arrington 1993:75) and the lack of scholarship on the subject, the regular use of models *in the teaching of composition* complicates this "official" position. Although designed to explore the extent to which first-year writing instructors address reading in their writing classrooms, the CCCC-funded and IRB-approved national study of first-year writing instructors I conducted as part of my book *Securing a Place for Reading in Composition: The Importance of Teaching for Transfer* (2015) also yielded other findings, as studies often do. Overall, 75 percent (n = 36) of the 48 percent of instructors who reported teaching rhetorical reading use "model," "example," or "sample" texts to do so. The students who agreed to participate in follow-up interviews often articulated this approach in detail. Sheryl described her course's readings from the textbook *Everything's an Argument* (Lunsford, Ruszkiewicz, and Walters 2016) as focused on different rhetorical strategies, noting that the textbook "talked about ethos, pathos, logos, and then kind of how to structure an argument. I feel like that was helpful in structuring my own argument and kind of making sure the reasoning was all sound, the evidence was all there" (Carillo 2015:38). Barbara experienced similar connections: "Our teacher point[ed] out particular rhetorical techniques that [authors] use and encourag[ed] us to use that . . . in our own writing" (Carillo 2015:38). Wanda described how her instructor encouraged the application of sentence-level modeling of the personal narratives they read: "I found some great phrases and great sentences that I mimic[ked] and [then] created my own" (Carillo 2015:38). Kaila described how she benefited at both the local and global level from the way her instructor connected the course's reading to writing: "We read and we use[d] it as an example or as an idea to incorporate into what we wr[ote]. We read an example in our textbooks of a memoir and we['d] use it as an example of how we should write our memoir . . . [This reading also] helped me see how proper grammar is used and how sentences should be constructed. It helped me a lot with that" (Carillo 2015:38). Although a bit skeptical about the reading for her course, Kaila said she "noticed reading, like the examples [the instructor] gave us to read . . . helped me write, so I decided that reading would help me write better" (Carillo 2015:38). As these excerpts from the interviews suggest, not only are instructors using models in their classrooms, but the models are having a positive effect on students' motivation to read since they overtly connect the reading for the course to the writing for the course.

Mike Bunn (2013:505) found something similar in his more local study of first-year writing instructors' teaching practices at the University of Michigan:

An important strategy for teaching reading-writing connections surfaced again and again as instructors answered a range of survey questions, and most notably in responses to the question How (if at all) do you teach a connection between reading and writing to students in first-year writing? Assigning model texts is discussed by 17 [out of 57] different instructors and referred to a total of 27 times throughout the surveys. These model texts—mostly published pieces, though sample student papers are occasionally mentioned as well—are primarily discussed in two different ways: as displays of writing techniques and strategies that students can identify and then try in their own writing, or as examples of the specific genre that students will eventually be assigned to write.

David Bartholomae and Beth Matway's (2010) study at the University of Pittsburgh also demonstrated that instructors *across the disciplines* are using models in the classroom:

> Many of those we interviewed use models in their teaching— either examples of student papers or examples of professional writing—in order to give students a point of reference for genre, format, and style. With models, students learn that writing comes from within a community rather than out of the blue (or through divine inspiration). In some cases, the models are provided only to those students who are struggling, who don't have a sense of what is expected of them or who need help in imagining "good" writing. The use of published models also prepares students to read the professional literature—not simply for information but as a demonstration of thought and method.

In addition to the findings from local and national studies that complicate composition's "official" position against imitation and modeling, so does the success of Gerald Graff and Cathy Birkenstein's (2015) *They Say/I Say: The Academic Moves That Matter in Academic Writing*. First published in 2005, the book is now in its third edition and boasts many versions, including some with readings and some without, as well as high school and college editions. The book gives students model sentences to imitate as well as templates, and students are expected to fill in the blanks of these templates and model sentences. Although its approach is controversial because of its connection to formalist pedagogies, the book is one of the most widely circulating handbooks on academic writing of all time.

And so this chapter's investment in modeling—in this case the modeling of sound reading practices—is not as provocative as it might seem at first. More important, though, this chapter is bringing the pedagogical practices of modeling and imitative exercises to the forefront, which allows for a reexamination of these practices and their potential uses. This is especially crucial since evidence from the studies mentioned above suggests that these are practices being used in composition classes across the country. Keeping these practices hidden from view, locked away in classrooms rather than openly discussed in the field's publications, does not provide support for those instructors already incorporating models into their pedagogy or resources for those who see the potential in these activities but have been led to believe that imitation is an antiquated pedagogy. The remainder of this chapter posits that incorporating models of annotation into one's pedagogy in order to teach practices of annotation can be an especially productive way of providing direct instruction in reading. To do so, we must think beyond imitative *writing* practices and consider what it might mean to model sound *reading* practices for our students. This chapter thus opens up opportunities for imagining how, in Farmer and Arrington's (1993) words, "imitation might be seriously rethought."

Exploring how the ancient practice of imitation might play a role in contemporary literacy instruction is especially appropriate not simply because our current political climate demands alternatives to widely circulating interpretive models that depend on decontextualization,[18] which annotation can mitigate, but because twenty-first-century multi-modal literacy practices have once again destabilized the notion of the (solitary, Romantic) author, one of the tenets on which the very rejection of imitation pedagogies depends. As we remain open to accepting more socially inflected definitions of authorship, this chapter contends that embracing more socially inflected iterations of reading can be a powerful way of supporting instruction in reading.

RECOVERING THE COMPLEXITY OF IMITATIVE EXERCISES

Bringing modeling out into the light, as does this chapter, allows us to recover some long-forgotten elements of imitation in classical rhetoric, "the single most common instructional method in the west for well over two millennia" (Muckelbauer 2008:52). "From the time of Gorgias until the middle of [the twentieth] century," writes John Muckelbauer (2008:52), "any student who received formal education at any level was almost certainly subjected to explicit exercises in imitation." These exercises were meant to help students develop their oratorical abilities, taste, and ethics. So as not to deviate too far from the focus of this chapter, I will limit my exploration of the uses of imitative pedagogies in classical rhetoric to Quintilian's *Institutio Oratorio*, since it details the most comprehensive educational program in classical rhetoric and spends significant time exploring the concept of imitation within this pedagogical framework.

The most relevant complexities that emerge when we revisit Quintilian's pedagogy have to do with the methods and goals of these pedagogical practices. Quintilian and other rhetoricians were not teaching imitation as a slavish method of copying but rather as a deliberate and critically inclined method of composition. In *Institutio Oratorio*, which was itself modeled after Cicero's works, Quintilian (2001) lays out various methods that will help students become better orators, including *lectio* (reading aloud), *praelectio* (analysis of a text), *memoria* (memorization of models), *paraphrasis* (paraphrasing of models), and *conversio* (transliteration), recitation, and correction (Murphy 2012). Quintilian addresses imitation throughout Book Ten of *Institutio Oratorio* and regularly challenges our contemporary notion of imitation as an act of submission: "First of all, then, imitation is not sufficient on its own. For one thing, only a lazy mind is content with what others have discovered" (2001:10.2.4). Later, he reminds his students, "And nothing does grow by imitation alone. But if we are not allowed to add to previous achievements, how can we hope for our ideal orator?" (10.2.8–9). Imitation as described by Quintilian is not about menial or subservient copying. It's about improving on the original. This involves considerable work on the part of the student, who must "first understand what it is that he is going to imitate, and to know why it is good" (10.2.18). From here, Quintilian makes an interesting move, particularly in light of contemporary theories of writing across the curriculum (WAC), in that he instructs his students that "each genre has its own law, and its own standard of appropriateness" (10.2.22) and warns students against "devot[ing] themselves to one particular manner" (10.2.22).

Andrew Bourelle (2009) convincingly reads these and other moments in Book Ten as anticipating the modern WAC movement, born in the 1970s. Read in this way, these moments also suggest that instructors need to help students develop the critical acumen to choose appropriate models for imitation. In fact, despite contemporary understandings of imitative exercises, Quintilian (2001) not only insists on instructing students about choosing the model most suited to their needs but also that students must be prepared to articulate why it is an appropriate model within the context in which they are working. Students, too, must find ways to surpass the model. In Muckelbauer's (2008:59) words, this is nothing short of "a massive analytical endeavor."

This quick gloss of Quintilian's approach to teaching imitation foregrounds the space he imagines between the model and the copy, a space that allows the student to go further, to do more, to improve on the model. Muckelbauer (2008) explores how this space between the model and the copy can facilitate invention because "variation" naturally enters into the process of imitation. This "variation," according to Muckelbauer (2008:63–64), is the result of a few different factors: "students' different individual natures and [their] imitation of various models, which necessarily results in the blending of specific qualities from different authors." Upsetting the common opposition between invention (i.e., creative genesis) and imitation, Muckelbauer argues that imitative exercises do not inherently or necessarily degrade creativity. As Muckelbauer points out, even when imitation is defined as repetition-of-the-same or reproduction, not only is pure imitation impossible, but in its impossibility it creates a space for invention.

CHOOSING MODELS OF ANNOTATION
FOR THE "NOVICE" READER

Finding and choosing models for writing students to emulate is a daunting task. But the recent uptick and interest in annotation and marginalia has made this a bit easier. Not only have periodicals been using annotation to provide "context and commentary" for their readers, as discussed above, but in 2015 there was an exhibition on annotation at the New York Society Library titled *Readers Make Their Mark*. Digital projects that track readers' commentary on texts, including *Book Traces* and *Annotated Books Online*, have also emerged, and annotated versions of the US Constitution and the Declaration of Independence were released in 2009. Moreover, Kindle's "popular highlights" and "public notes" features allow readers to see which passages other readers have highlighted and commented on, and Niemanstoryboard.org has introduced a feature called "Annotation Tuesday" in which one writer interviews another writer and the interview itself includes interspersed annotations from both writers that document their reactions and related commentary. These and other models of annotation—both digital and print—are more widely available than ever before. While these publicly available annotated texts may not contain the specific disciplinary bent an instructor would be looking for, they serve as "evidence that reading is a constructive act" (Bartholomae and Petrosky 1986:16). As such, they can lay the foundation for discussions about reading as a complex, active process that will help prepare students to be active participants in their chosen disciplines.

I imagine that while all instructors are generally committed to helping prepare our students to be active participants in our fields, asking them to engage in exercises dependent on imitation, which can connote passivity, may not necessarily seem like a productive route. I would posit, though, that we can cast the relationship between the student and her model in a more positive light if we think about the relationship between the creator of the model and the student as one between a novice and an expert, in much the same way the relationship between teacher and student is cast in Quintilian's and other rhetoricians' teachings. In this scenario, novice students are still learning about the conventions and expectations associated with reading in their chosen fields while the models of readings (i.e., the annotations) have been developed by expert readers in those fields.

As Alice Horning (2011) has pointed out, there has been a significant amount of research on the development of expertise generally, as well as specifically about developing expert literacy practices. Although Horning does not address the use of models in her own scholarship, she outlines the reading practices of experts so instructors can help their students, novice readers, develop these practices. Drawing on research from educational psychology conducted by Maria Scardamalia and Carl Brereiter (1991) as well as Ruth Clark (2008), Horning (2011) describes how experts are able to "apply teachable and learnable strategies to achieve comprehension of the text itself . . . along with skimming, scanning and adjustments to speed." Moreover, explains Horning, drawing on Clark, "expertise arises from extended, deliberate practice within the domain or area that is of interest to the learner." When experts get stuck, they draw on their experience and what Clark (2008:13) calls "adaptive expertise," which is the ability to remain flexible and integrate that prior experience and expertise into a new situation, to adapt it in a way that allows experts to become "unstuck." Novices, in contrast, tend to lack strategies for comprehending texts and are not particularly adept at making adjustments to how they read because they lack the reflective capacity to judge when doing so is necessary. Moreover, when novices get stuck, they often lack the strategies to get unstuck, particularly if they view reading as an exercise in "getting the right meaning." As Bartholomae and Petrosky (1986:18) point out, students often "believe that difficulty in reading is a sign of a problem, either their's or the book's, and not a sign that there is some work for the reader to do." If a student does attempt to surmount that difficulty, instead of returning to a text that has been annotated, as would likely be the case with an experienced reader, the novice reader often returns to a blank text "and so a rereading stands only as the act of going back again to an empty text—to read it again; this time, they hope, to get it right" (Bartholomae and Petrosky 1986:18).

Bartholomae's description of the novice reader seems to also suggest a lack of purpose for reading—beyond "getting it right." Founding director of the Office of Teaching Effectiveness and Innovation at Clemson University and author of *Teaching at Its Best: A Research-Based Resource for College Instructors* Linda B. Nilson (2015) has pointed this out as a key difference between novice and expert readers. Unlike "expert readers," students often fail to read with a purpose. As experts read, explains Nilson (2015), they are "looking for something that's useful and important to [their] work. Students often tackle assigned readings with no purpose at all." Based on their extensive research on students' reading and writing practices, Richard Haas and Linda Flower (1988:182) noted: "While experienced readers may understand that both reading and writing are context-rich, situational, constructive acts, many students see reading and writing as merely information exchange: knowledge telling when they write, and 'knowledgegetting' when they read." In her own research, Linda Flower (1990:6) explained that the "distinction between reading to compose and reading to do something else matters because different purposes push the reading process into distinctive shapes." As such, when choosing disciplinary models of reading, instructors need to be cognizant of why they are asking their students to read.

Until instructors figure out why they are asking their students to read, they will not be able to find appropriate models that best suit those purposes. They cannot, in other words, adequately prepare their students to read purposefully. Keith Hjortshoj (2009:125, emphasis in original) points out that while instructors can often be heard claiming that students don't know how to read, what they are really commenting on is students' inability to read with purpose: "The impression that college students do not know *how* to read usually results from the fact that they do not know *why* they are reading assigned texts. This lack of purpose, in turn, results from the way that reading is typically assigned in undergraduate courses: as an undifferentiated, solitary activity to be completed for the vague purpose of knowing what the text contains."

David Jolliffe and Allison Harl's (2008) study of first-year students' reading habits at the University of Arkansas further corroborates Hjortshoj's argument. The data Jolliffe and Harl (2008:613) collected, in the form of questionnaires, journals, and exit interviews about students' reading habits including their personal reading and school-based reading for all their courses, suggested that students were unsure of why they were reading for their classes. Even with the researchers' "leading prompts," students "rarely made the kinds of connections that lead to engaged reading, particularly text-to-world and text-to-text connections." Moreover, Jolliffe and Harl (2008:612) indicated that they would be "hard pressed to find reading experiences [they] would characterize as focused and contemplative." "Students were reading," noted Jolliffe and Harl (2008:611), "but they were not reading studiously." As such, they recommend that instructors "explain explicitly to students how the documents that they must read relate directly to the aims and methods of learning that are most valued in the course environment, show clearly how students' reading for the course should be manifest in projects and examinations, and demonstrate specifically *how* students should read the course material" (Jolliffe and Harl 2008:614, emphasis in original). I would posit that this is necessary especially when assigning model texts. Instructors cannot assume that students will recognize the readings as models, something Bunn (2013) and Smagorinsky (1992) realized in their own studies.

That direct instruction can come in many forms. Although they don't call it such, Jolliffe and Harl recommend modeling reading. Unlike this chapter, though, which encourages the use of annotations for doing so, Jolliffe and Harl (2008:613) recommend the use of think-aloud protocols: "As they read, students need to be walked through demonstrations of mature, committed, adult readers who draw connections to the world around them, both historical and current, and to other texts . . . The instructor simply focuses on a passage—say, 250 words or so—from the required reading and reads it aloud to student[s], pausing regularly to explain to the students what connections he or she is making to his or her own life and work, to the world beyond the text, and, most important, to other texts that he or she has read."

Jolliffe and Harl's (2008) description of "mature, committed, adult readers" references students' inability to move beyond what Jolliffe and Harl characterize as an immature dependence on text-to-self connections. We might substitute "expert readers" for "mature, committed, adult readers" to further crystallize the comparison they make. John Bean (2011:137) suggests a similar strategy for instructors: "You might take some class time to discuss with students your own reading processes. One approach is to create little research scenarios to help students see how and why your reading strategies vary." If Louis Menand (2009) is right that "teachers are the books that students read most closely," then we might as well use this to our advantage and model the kind of reading we want our students to perform.

As instructive as read-aloud protocols are in giving students access to what it looks like when an expert reads, using sample annotations gives students something physical to which they can return. Unfortunately, think-aloud protocols are as elusive as reading itself; when the demonstration is over, there is no way to return to it. By definition, annotations leave marks, allowing students to return to them for support as they work toward becoming expert readers in their fields. In the following section I describe my use of model annotations in one of my own courses as a means to provide direct instruction in reading.

EXPERIMENTING WITH MODEL ANNOTATIONS
IN A RESEARCH WRITING COURSE

At the University of Connecticut I teach a course called Writing through Research, a sophomore-level interdisciplinary research writing course intended to serve as a bridge between students' required first-year writing course and the writing-intensive course they will take in their major. The course helps students meet the university's "writing competency" requirement, although it is an elective that is not required by the general education program and it does not meet any content requirements for graduation. I teach the course annually, and it is usually composed of a mix of students from a range of majors and standings, despite its position in the curriculum as a 2000-level course. The course itself uses modeling on many different levels and in various ways. I divide the course into two halves, so to speak. The first half is spent as an entire class working together on a source-driven essay about literacy and technology wherein I teach the traditional components of composing a research essay: developing a research question, reading sources, synthesizing sources, documenting sources, and writing, editing, and revising the essay. Although I supply the sources and the general topic for this first essay—the effect of what Sven Birkerts (1994) calls "electronic culture" on the humans who interact with it—students must choose which sources of those I assigned they will use and what specific aspect of that general topic they will explore. In the second half of the course, when students develop their own topic to explore, they are expected to apply what they learned about that process in the first half. For this second essay, which will be revised and then also developed into a short oral presentation, students are invited to pose a question about any topic they like. I encourage them to continue working on a question raised but not pursued in another course, a topic of personal relevance to them, or a topic that emerges from their field.

The most challenging aspects of the course do not come from having to stay up to speed on the various documentation practices my students from all disciplines will be using or the range of preparations students from all levels bring with them but from students' tendency to write research *reports*, to simply report and (re)present their research rather than do anything with it. The "learning culture of demand" (Perkins and Salomon 2012:257), mentioned above, has encouraged this approach to source-based writing, and as Bruce Ballenger (1997:97) has pointed out, the "conventional research paper" emphasizes "mastering formal conventions and accumulating evidence to make a point." While I want students to become aware of the conventions (formal and otherwise) that govern their writing within their disciplines, this particular course encourages instructors to teach writing as an inquiry-driven practice. As such, I am constantly trying to balance instruction in the Montaignian essay—which values exploration, inquiry, and open-endedness—and an introduction to the different conventions and values associated with the range of disciplines represented by my students each semester. My students seem to recognize my struggle as they, too, struggle to understand what I am asking for in relation to the more traditional research reports to which they have become accustomed. "I am having trouble grasping how you can turn a research paper into your own analysis, as all of the research papers I've done have been systematic reviews or compiling sources to discuss a topic of my choice," wrote one student in an email as she worked toward writing the open-topic research essay for the course. The student's references to "systematic reviews" and "compiling sources" corroborate Ballenger's (1997:97) research that describes research papers as exercises in "accumulating evidence" as opposed to analyzing sources.

I have tried to deal with this and related challenges by foregrounding mindful reading. Because I believe mindful reading is so crucial to strong writing—particularly source-based writing—students spent the first three weeks of the course focusing on and practicing different reading strategies, including annotation, within the mindful reading framework. Still, I eventually realized that I needed to be more explicit about my use of models. I was assigning readings that were largely indicative of the kind of writing in which I wanted students to engage, but, like the instructors in Bunn's (2013) and Smagorinsky's (1992) studies, I was not doing enough to situate them as such. I was not teaching students how to read them in order to imitate them in the ways I had hoped they would so they could move beyond merely reporting in their essays. I fell into that common trap: I told students what I didn't want— a report—but I wasn't as explicit as I might have been about what I *did* want. Although still a fairly new revision of my teaching, I have begun doing more than simply assigning these readings. I have begun situating these readings—and one in particular, discussed below—as models of the kind of essays I would like students to write. Moreover, and most important for this chapter, I have also begun modeling *the kind of reading* that will help them write that essay.

Richard Miller's teaching at Rutgers University has served as a crucial resource in articulating to my students what I *do* want from them in their reading and writing. Miller's description of the final assignment in his Reading in Slow Motion course at Rutgers captures what I want students to accomplish in their research essays. In his article about that course, titled "Digital Reading," Miller (2016) describes his students' final essay assignment. He wants students to compose "an essay that meditates, speculates, deliberates, explores. The work of such an essay is to open a question up and to keep it open for as long as possible, so that connections between the question and other issues can come to light. Your final project will be assessed on what it does. Have you used your writing to extend your thinking? To explore complexity? To generate insight and understanding?" (Miller 2016:162).

While giving Miller credit for this description, I use this language in my own class so that I am totally explicit about the kind of writing I expect (see appendix 4.a for the assignment). To prepare students to undertake this kind of writing—very different from what has been asked of them in other courses—I offer them two kinds of models. The first model is an exploratory essay called "MahVuhHuhPuh" by Sven Birkerts (1994), which is one of the readings students complete at the beginning of the semester but that I had never previously situated as a model (although I had hoped they would emulate it). Interestingly, Birkerts models his writing after Virginia Woolf's writing, a point he makes in the essay's opening pages. As such, students see firsthand how imitation (in this case as a form of paying homage to Woolf's exploratory method) might be employed among professional, published authors. The second model is the model of reading, the annotated version of Birkerts's piece that I distribute to students late in the semester just before they compose their first submission of their research essay. Using Bunn's Reading Like a Writer strategy, with which my students are familiar, I annotate the first five pages of Birkerts's essay. The purpose of these annotations is to model for students how one would read to develop a deeper understanding of *how* Birkerts writes, the moves he makes so his piece remains exploratory and inquiry-driven. I emphasize here that I offer my own annotations (albeit just the first five pages of the text) as a model of expert annotations; instructors need not be overwhelmed by the prospect of looking beyond themselves to provide "expert" annotations. I have included a copy of those "expert" annotations in appendix 4.a.[19] The first five pages of Birkerts's essay are, unfortunately, not as representative of the rich writerly techniques he uses as the essay progresses wherein there are many more opportunities for students to notice how Birkerts uses the kinds of techniques Bunn (2013) addresses in his essay.

With Bunn's Reading Like a Writer (RLW) strategy in mind, as well as several pages of my own annotations, students are asked to reread Birkerts's piece for the "writerly choices" (a term Bunn uses) he makes. They are instructed to consider how they may incorporate some of the same moves into their own writing to compose a research essay that is "genuinely exploratory" (Ballenger 1997:97). The difference between students' more generalized annotations from the beginning of the semester and their Reading Like a Writer annotations was that the latter were directly connected to a specific writing assignment. When they were (re)reading like a writer, they were not paying attention to the content of Birkerts's piece but to its form, how he does what he does so they can do the same. They make his writerly choices visible through their reading, which is concretized through the practice of annotation.

In their reflections on their essays, students describe the various elements they notice while annotating Birkerts's piece in this way, elements they often then work to incorporate in their own essays. In response to this assignment, one student writes, "I noticed . . . he had a clear thought pattern [and] I attempted to imitate a thought process [in my essay]." Another describes how Birkerts "lingered on literally every single thing he said." A third student writes that Birkerts showed her "how someone can glide through the planes of introspection smoothly . . . reminding [her] of the methods of puzzling things together." Students regularly remark on Birkerts's conversational tone and use of personal experience: "I noticed that he relied on a lot of anecdotes and personal experience while talking to the reader by using 'I,' 'we,' and 'us.'" Others notice how often he poses questions: "I noticed his questioning. I wanted to talk in the first-person and [ask] questions like him. I made a conscious effort to ask questions, make myself more relevant to the conversation." Overall, the essays written by the students quoted just above (and other students not quoted) are stronger than those essays I received in the semesters in which I did not carve out time to model for students how to make these observations while reading. They are stronger in that students are more willing to linger on ideas, raise questions, consider the relevance of their subject to themselves and others, and write in a less stilted way. Anthony R. Petrosky (1982) found something similar when he pushed his students to draw on the personal to demonstrate how they constructed meaning from the assigned texts. This approach gave students "a way to flesh out the personal knowledge that informed their comprehension, they were better able to explain themselves to each other . . . I do think that this kind of elaboration and explanation is a necessary beginning to more critical examinations of texts and the assumptions underlying readers' readings of them" (Petrosky 1982:34).

Like Quintilian and his fellow classical rhetoricians, I expect students to produce essays that on some level are even stronger than Birkerts's model essay but that, like his, draw overtly on the personal knowledge that informs their chosen line of inquiry. In part because I didn't want students to get hung up on simply "accumulating evidence" (Ballenger 1997:97), I chose a model essay that really doesn't provide much in the way of evidence, something to which students (at least in some classes I have taught) immediately object. These students critique Birkerts for using only anecdotal evidence to make grand claims about American culture and its relationship to technology. And so a space emerges for them to do better than Birkerts, to find some evidence that supports and helps them explore and develop their line of inquiry. Still, because they must use Birkerts's essay as a model, they are not accumulating evidence as the traditional "research paper" might encourage. That said, they must find ways of incorporating evidence into an exploratory piece that while remaining focused on its subject also, in Birkerts's (1994:13) own words, represents "a kind of narrative travel that allows for picnics along the way" so that "connections between the question and other issues can come to light" (Miller 2016:162).

Students' focus on Birkerts's form—through the act of annotation—allows them to get at something even bigger than form and writerly choices, something that seems even more important today than it has been in the past. Birkerts's Montaignian (or Woolfian) form models for students what it looks like to "open a question up and to keep it open for as long as possible" (Miller 2016:162) rather than to rush to judgment. When students annotate Birkerts's piece, they notice this—Birkerts "lingered on literally every single thing he said," as one student quoted above observed (or perhaps complained). This form models a way of thinking, of engaging, and of being in the world, a way of being that is characterized by slow, careful deliberation and a commitment to curiosity and openness.

This form models a relationship to the world that John Duffy (2017) recently described in his keynote address at the University of Connecticut's twelfth annual conference on the teaching of writing. Duffy told the story of a student he called Christine whose family, living in northern Wisconsin in the 1990s, was embroiled in "a clash of cultures" wherein white sports fisherman and resort owners and members of the Native American Ojibwe tribe fought over the tribe's rights to hunt and fish off-reservation, including to spearfish walleye during the spawning season. Angered by "what they regarded as 'special rights' to use spearfishing methods that were illegal for other fishermen, the white fisherman and resort owners would gather at the lakes where the Ojibwe fished, shouting racial slurs, throwing rocks at Ojibwe fishermen, launching speedboats, and circling the Ojibwe boats at high speed, attempting to swamp them. Riot police were eventually called in to maintain order" (Duffy 2017:13–14). A daughter of a resort owner, Christine "felt that her father and other resort owners were being hurt economically, and she resented the media representations, as she saw it, of the white resort owners and fishermen as racists. Christine decided she would write about the controversy" (Duffy 2017:14), and she planned to do so (not surprisingly) from the point of view of the white resort owners. But in the midst of the process she approached Duffy, wanting to change her thesis. She told him that "she would continue to argue that the resort owners had legitimate grievances, as the tribal fishing practices threatened their livelihoods. But she had been reading, she said, and thinking about what she read. She now wanted to argue that the Ojibwe, too, had legitimate claims, and their traditional practices should be respected. Her new thesis would call for an accommodation of some kind" (Duffy 2017:14).

Duffy (2017:14–15) compellingly described this as a pivotal moment in Christine's writing process, and he went on to talk about "the admiration [he] felt for . . . her intellectual courage—her willingness to look at contrary points of view, to take them seriously, and, in the end, to expand her ways of thinking about a problem that affected her and her family directly." As I listened, though, I heard something different. Yes, this was undoubtedly a pivotal moment for Christine, but it was a moment, at least as Duffy represented it, in which reading—not writing—was the catalyst. "But she had been reading, she said, and thinking about what she read," explained Duffy (2017:15). It was her reading—not her writing—that led her to "look at contrary points of view, to take them seriously, and in the end [to] expand her ways of thinking" (Duffy 2017:15). It was reading that shifted Christine's relationship to the text and to her world. Who knows if Christine annotated what she read. It doesn't much matter if she used that tool or some other that allowed her, an otherwise shy student as described by Duffy, to respond to her reading with such openness. Despite how negatively affected (financially and otherwise) she thought her family was and would continue to be by the Ojibwe, Christine's way of reading led her to revise her thesis to call for accommodations for that very group.

It seems that "Christines" are few and far between today, and I don't just mean in our classrooms. Happy to reside in our own echo chambers, we are largely loathe to listen to and be swayed by opposing points of view (a subject that will be picked up in chapter 5), and fewer of us still are open to the sort of transformation Christine experienced. But I do think that if we make visible the role of reading in the writing process, as I have tried to do with Duffy's anecdote just above, we can better position our students to respond to the word and the world in this way. Students need to be supported in this process so they can fill in the gaps in their ways of reading. In the end, it wasn't simply that Christine "had been reading," as Duffy (2017:14) notes, but that she had been *reading in a particular way*. Christine was reading as an expert reads—she was reading in open and flexible ways that allowed her to incorporate the new information she was encountering into her existing framework. Rather than ignore the dissonance between what Christine grew up thinking about the Ojibwe and what she was now learning through reading, Christine adjusted her way of thinking to incorporate that new information. Most students, though, need more support than Christine to move them toward the expert models that will allow them to contribute most productively to their chosen fields as well as to a democracy that depends on citizens' open-mindedness and willingness to compromise. Annotation is a concrete tool to support this important work.

APPENDIX 4.A
Writing through Research: Preparation for the Open-Topic Research Essay

Last class we discussed that for the final essay you should not write a research *report* but instead a research essay that, in the words of Richard E. Miller (2016:162), "meditates, speculates, deliberates, explores." As Miller (2016:162) explains, "The work of such an essay is to open a question up and to keep it open for as long as possible, so that connections between the question and other issues can come to light." I will assess your essay on what it does, how you use your research and writing to extend your thinking, to explore complexity, and to generate insight and understanding (Miller 2016:162). You'll recall that during this class I also described Sven Birkerts's "MahVuhHuhPuh" (1994) as an exemplar of this type of essay.

In preparation for writing this kind of essay, please review the annotated pages of "MahVuhHuhPuh" I distributed. Notice how these annotations pay attention to what Birkerts does (as opposed to what he says). Another way to access what Birkerts does is to apply the "reading like a writer" strategy we previously discussed. A short reading by Mike Bunn about this strategy is posted on HUSKY CT for your review. Prior to composing the first submission of your essay, please annotate Birkerts's essay by "reading like a writer" to focus specifically on what he *does* and *how* he does it.

WORK CITED

Miller, Richard E. 2016. "On Digital Reading." *Pedagogy: Critical Approaches to Teaching Literature, Language, Composition, and Culture* 16 (1): 153–64. https://doi.org/10.1215/15314200-3158717.

MahVuhHuhPuh

IT WAS VIRGINIA WOOLF who started me thinking about thinking again. set me to weighing the relative merits of the abstract analytical mode against the attractions of a more oblique and subjective approach. The comparison was ventured for interest alone. Abstract analysis has been closed to me for some time—I find I can no longer chase the isolated haze. Problems and questions seem to come toward me in clusters. They appear inextricably imbedded in circumstance and I cannot pry them loose to think about them. Nor can I help factoring in my own angle of regard. All is relative, relational, Einsteinian. Thinking is now something I partake in, not something I do. It is a complex narrative proposition, and I am as interested in the variables of the process as I am in the outcome. I am an essayist, it seems, and not a philosopher.

I have had these various distinctions in mind for some time now, but only as a fidgety scatter of inklings. The magnet that pulled them into a shape was Woolf's classic essay, *A Room of One's Own*. Not the what of it, but the *how*. Reading the prose, I confronted a paradox that pulled me upright in my chair. Woolf's ideas are, in fact, few and fairly obvious—at least from our historical vantage. Yet the *thinking*, the presence of animate thought on the page, is striking. How do we sort that? How can a piece of writing have simple ideas and still infect the reader with the excitement of its thinking? The answer, I'd say, is that ideas are not the sum and substance of thought; rather, thought is as much about the motion across the water as it is about the stepping stones that allow it. It is an intricate choreography of movement, transition, and repose, a revelation of the musculature of mind. And this, abundantly and exalt-

ingly, is what I find in Woolf's prose. She supplies the context, shows the problem as well as her relation to it. Then, as she narrates her growing engagement, she exposes something more thrilling and valuable than any mere concept could be. She reveals how incidental experience can encounter the receptive sensibility and activate the mainspring of creativity.

I cannot cite enough text here to convince you of my point, but I can suggest the flavor of her musing, her particular way of intertwining the speculative with the reportorial. Woolf has, she informs us at the outset, beguiled to present her views on the subject of women and fiction. In the early pages of her essay she rehearses her own perplexity. She is a writer looking for an idea. What she does is not so very different from the classic college freshman maneuver of writing a paper on the problem she is having writing a paper. But Woolf is Woolf, and her stylistic verve is unexcelled.

Here then I was (call me Mary Beton, Mary Seton, Mary Carmichael or by any name you please—it is not a matter of any importance) sitting on the banks of a river a week or two ago in fine October weather, lost in thought. That collar I have spoken of, women and fiction, the need of coming to some conclusion on a subject that raises all sorts of prejudices and passions, bowed my head to the ground. To the right and left bushes of some sort, golden and crimson, glowed with color, even it seemed burned with the heat, of fire. On the further bank the willows wept in perpetual lamentation, their hair about their shoulders. The river reflected whatever it chose of sky and bridge and burning tree, and when the undergraduate had oared his boat through the reflections they closed again, completely, as if he had never been. There one might have sat the clock round lost in thought. Thought—to call it by a prouder name than it deserved—let its line down into the stream. It swayed, minute after minute, hither and thither among the reflections and the weeds, letting the water lift it and sink it, until—you know the little tug—the sudden conglomeration of an idea at the end of one's line; and then the cautious hauling of it in, and the careful laying of it out? Alas, laid on the grass how small, how insignificant this thought of mine looked; the sort of fish that a good fisherman puts back into the

watered that it may grow fatter and be one day worth cooking and eating.

Soon enough, Woolf will rise and attempt to cross a patch of lawn, only to encounter a zealous beadle, who will not only shoo her back toward authorized turf, but will initiate her reverie on male power and privilege. This is her triumph: the trust in serendipity, which proves, when unmasked, to be an absolute faith in the transformative powers of the creative intellect. *A Room of One's Own*, whatever it says about women, men, writing, and society, is also a perfect demonstration of what might be called "magpie aesthetics." Woolf is the bricoleuse, cobbling with whatever is to hand; she is the flaneuse, redeeming the slight and incidental by creating the context of its true significance. She models another path for mind and sensibility, suggests procedures that we might consider implementing for ourselves now that the philosophers, the old lovers of truth, have followed the narrowing track of abstraction to the craggy places up above the timberline.

By now the astute reader will have picked up on my game—that I am interested not only in celebrating Woolf's exemplary sidelong approach, but that I am trying, in my own ungainly way, to imitate it. Woolf had her "collar" (women and fiction) thrust upon her; I have wriggled into mine—let's call it *reading and meaning*—of my own volition. I know that I face an impossible task. Who can hope to say anything conclusive on so vast a subject? But I opted for vastness precisely because it would allow me to explore this unfamiliar essayistic method. A method predicated not upon conclusiveness but upon exploratory digressiveness: a method which proposes that thinking is not simply utilitarian, but can also be a kind of narrative travel that allows for picnics along the way.

I invoke Woolf as the instigating presence. Her example sets the key signature for an inquiry into the place of reading and sensibility in what is becoming an electronic culture. Within the scheme I have in mind, Woolf stands very much at one limit. Indeed, her work is an emblem for some of the very things that are under threat in our just differentiated subjectivity, reverie, verbal articulation, mental passage...

Before I go on, I must make a paradoxical admission. I was spurred

Continued on next page

to read *A Room of One's Own* by watching a televised adaptation of the book. On the program, Eileen Atkins, playing the part of Woolf, soliloquized for a full hour. Her address, supposedly directed at an audience of women at Girton College, was composed of extracted passages from the text. Around with minimal props and a rather extraordinary repertoire of gestures, Atkins held forth. And I, wedged into my corner of the couch, was mesmerized. By the acting, sure, but more by the sheer power and beauty of the spoken word. Here, without seeming archaic or excessively theatrical, was a language such as one never hears—certainly not on TV. I was riveted. And as soon as the show was over I went to find the book.

A Room of One's Own, I'm happy to say, stood up to its television rendition—indeed, galloped right past it. And it has spent many nights since on my bedside table. But the paradox remains: Just as Woolf's charged prose shows us what is possible with language, so it also forces us to face the utter impoverishment of our own discourse. And as we seek to explain how it is that flatness and dullness carry the day, we have to lay at least part of the blame at the feet of our omnipotent media systems. And yet, and yet ... here I found myself reintroduced to the power of Woolf by the culprit technology itself.

This is the sort of thing I tend to think about. I ponder the paradox—stare at it as if it were an object on the desk in front of me. I stare and wait for ideas and intuitions to gather, but I do not unpack my arguments of reason. For, as I see it, this little triad—of me, TV, and book—potentially touches every aspect of our contemporary lives and our experience of meaning. To think about the rather analytically would be to break the filaments of the web.

I will therefore set down what amount to a few anecdotal provocations and go wandering about in their midst. All of my points of focus have, as you will see, some connection to my immediate daily experience; they are embedded in the context of my life. But they also have a discernible link. For I have been going around for quite some time with a single question—a single imprecisely general question—in my mind. The interrogation mark has been turned upside down and, to follow Woolf, lowered into the waters of my ordinary days. It is always there and, from time to time, for whatever reason, it captures the attention of

14

some swimming thing. I feel a tug: The paper is produced, the note gets scribbled, and the hook is thrown back out.

The question, again, is, "What is the place of reading, and of the reading sensibility, in our culture as it has become?" And, like most of the questions I ponder seriously, this one has been around long enough to have become a conspicuous topographical feature of my mental landscape. In my lifetime I have witnessed and participated in what amounts to a massive shift, a wholesale transformation of what I think of as the age-old ways of being. The primary human relations—to space, time, nature, and to other people—have been subjected to a warping pressure that is something new under the sun. Those who argue that the very nature of history is change—that change is constant—are missing the point. Our era has seen an escalation of the rate of change so drastic that all possibilities of evolutionary accommodation have been short-circuited. The advent of the computer and the astonishing sophistication achieved by our electronic communications media have together turned a range of isolated changes into something systemic. The way that people experience the world has altered more in the last fifty years than in the many centuries preceding ours. The eruptions in the early part of our century—the rise of world wars and emergent modernity—were premonitional of a sort. Since World War II we have stepped, collectively, out of an ancient and familiar solitude and into an enormous web of imponderable linkages. We have created the technology that not only enables us to change our basic nature, but that is making such change all but inevitable. This is why I take reading—reading construed broadly—as my subjects. Reading, for me, is one activity that inscribes the limit of the old conception of the individual and his relation to the world. It is precisely where reading leaves off, where it is supplanted by other modes of processing and transmitting experience, that the new dispensation can be said to begin.

None of this, I'm afraid, will seem very obvious to the citizen of the late twentieth century. If it did, there would be more outcry, more debate. The changes are keyed to generational transitions in computational power; they come in ghostly increments, but their effect is to alter our lives on every front. Public awareness of this expresses itself obliquely, often unconsciously, as nostalgia—a phenomenon which the

15

5
MOVING FORWARD

In previous chapters of this book, I have argued that rhetoric and composition has numerous resources to address many of the issues that are a result of living in a post-truth culture. In particular, as I have pointed out, teaching critical reading alongside writing will be crucial to this response. This chapter does not deny the importance of these resources and pedagogical approaches. Instead, as it exposes some of the field's foundational values and principles, this chapter explores how these, as well as some gaps in the field, may complicate our response. Anticipating and understanding the obstacles that may lie ahead is crucial to strengthening that response. As background for this exploration, I describe the very divisiveness that has helped me recognize the complications we, as a field, are likely to encounter.

THE DIVISIVENESS IN OUR POST-TRUTH CULTURE

Although the 2016 election seemed to have created an even greater divide between Democrats and Republicans, writer, lecturer, and broadcaster Kenan Malik (2016) describes the divide among the American people not as one between the ideologies of the left and right but as one even more fragmented than that and "shaped more by identity than by ideology":

> The key fault line today is not between left and right but between those who welcome a more globalized, technocratic world, and those who feel left out, dispossessed and voiceless. Mr. Trump's supporters and his liberal critics fall on different sides of this new divide. Many Trump supporters see their economic precariousness and political voicelessness as a result of globalization

DOI: 10.7330/9781607327912.c005

and immigration. They see it, too, as a cultural loss, turning, like many other groups in America, to the language of identity to express their discontent. Many liberals see such voters as "deplorables." Both sides interpret facts and news through their own particular political and cultural frames. All this has led to anguished discussions about people living in "echo chambers"—sealed-off social worlds in which the only views they hear are ones echoing their own.

Social media, of course, only perpetuates the growth of these "sealed-off social worlds" and exacerbates their consequences.[20] As Farhad Manjoo (2017) explains in the *New York Times*, "With its huge reach [2 billion people use Facebook every month], Facebook has begun to act as the great disseminator of the larger cloud of misinformation and half-truths swirling about the rest of media. It sucks up lies from cable news and Twitter, then precisely targets each lie to the partisan bubble most receptive to it." In fact, explains Majoo, "After studying how people shared 1.25 million stories during the [2016 presidential campaign], a team of researchers at M.I.T. and Harvard implicated Facebook and Twitter in the larger failure of media in 2016."

This chapter maintains that our field is up against more than social media and that we should be cautious as we move forward. Some of our field's values will necessarily pose unique challenges to our plight; moreover, there are also some major gaps in our knowledge. For example, as a field we have a deep understanding of both classical rhetoric and more contemporary rhetorical theories (many of which we have developed ourselves), but we lack a deep understanding of how persuasion works at the psychological level, both cognitively and emotionally. Moreover, while we promote reflection on one's own values and ideas, as well as careful and responsible engagement of those who oppose our own, we know little about the psychological demands that inform this work.

This chapter makes explicit some of these gaps within our field, as well as a handful of otherwise implicit values that I believe are particularly relevant to our response to this post-truth culture. In drawing attention to the values listed below, I intend to emphasize that they are not natural but constructed. Perhaps more important than simply exposing and examining them is our willingness as a field to revisit and revise them.

1. AS A FIELD, WE PRIVILEGE LOGOS AND OVERSIMPLIFY THE RELATIONSHIP BETWEEN LOGOS AND PATHOS

With roots in ancient Rhetoric, the field of rhetoric and composition and its professional organizations are "committed to promoting and teaching ethical rhetoric and writing [and] have viewed this rhetorical watershed moment as a direct challenge to their missions" (McComiskey 2017:3–4). Neglecting the traditional role of logos in rhetoric, those using and disseminating this post-truth political discourse are instead relying on—and abusing—ethos and pathos. As Bruce McComiskey (2017:33) points out in *Post-Truth Rhetoric and Composition*, this post-truth rhetoric "is based on . . . ethos and pathos parading as logos . . . the effects of all of this post-truth rhetoric . . . are anger, fear, angst, and violence." To insist that appeals to logic and rationality are the most valid responses to the degradation of logic is to think too narrowly about the complex issues at hand. As a field, we need to be open to reexamining our values and determing to what extent they will continue to serve us well.

Research from the field of psychology offers insight into the relationships among mental functions. Most striking in the psychological research on how people are persuaded is the degree to which emotion and beliefs are bound up with one another, intertwined, and thought to be largely inseparable. This complicates attempts to separate out—in order to prioritize—logos. In 2000 Nico H. Frijda, Antony S.R. Manstead, and Sacha Bem published a collection of essays on this very topic: *Emotions and Beliefs: How Feelings Influence Thoughts*. In their introduction they describe the recent evolution of "cognitive emotion theory," which has spawned "appraisal theory," a body of research that maintains that "emotions result from how the individual believes the world to be, how events are believed to have come about, and what implications events are believed to have" (Frijda, Manstead, and Ben 2000:1). Beliefs, then, are "one of the major determinants of emotion, and therefore an important part of the study of emotion" (Frijda, Manstead, and Bem 2000:1). If we are teaching our students how to think and read critically, we must educate ourselves on theories like cognitive emotion theory that recognize and explore the relationship between beliefs and emotion.

Emotions and Beliefs goes beyond more commonplace, mainstream iterations of the relationship between emotions and beliefs that often only consider how emotions might "distort" thinking. Instead, Frijda, Manstead, and Bem (2000:3) note that emotions affect beliefs in such varied and profound ways because "these effects are in fact central to the place of both emotions and beliefs in human functioning. It can be argued that they are in no way restricted to belief distortions. They are at the heart of what beliefs are about." As Frijda, Manstead, and Bem (2000:4) point out, though, in order to examine the relationship between emotions and beliefs, one must define them "in such a way that they can be treated as distinct and separate phenomena. This task is problematic, though, since emotions and beliefs are both mental states. They share certain qualities and they can be distinguished in terms of other attributes, but like all mental states, they are closely intertwined. Mental states evoke other mental states and together they form such an intricate web that distinctions become blurred."

In fact, in reviewing the literature on the relationship between thought and emotion, some of which is discussed in chapter 3, I was especially surprised to see how language that I (and others, I think) typically associate with thought and logos is used to describe emotion: Gerald Clore and Karen Gasper (2000), for example, describe the main function of emotion as providing information and guiding attention. Moreover, whereas we might assume that beliefs are largely responsible for leading to new beliefs, Nico Frijda and Batja Mesquita (2000:45–46) describe how emotions can both spawn new beliefs and strengthen existing ones.

Psychologist Jonathan Haidt has done several studies that show how emotions often do the work we normally associate with thinking or beliefs. Based on findings from several experiments indicating that people cannot articulate or provide evidence for why they believe what they believe, which Haidt coins "moral dumbfounding," Haidt (2001:821–22) concludes that "the roots of human intelligence, rationality, and ethical sophistication should not be sought in our ability to search for and evaluate evidence in an open and unbiased way. Rather than follow the ancient Greeks in worshipping reason, we should instead look for the roots of human intelligence, rationality, and virtue in what the mind does best: perception, intuition, and other mental operations that are quick, effortless, and generally quite accurate." In fact, Haidt's research seeks to privilege modes of thought that are based on intuition over those based on rationality.

Although controversial,[21] Haidt's theories must not be ignored, an argument philosopher Michael P. Lynch (2016:51) made before the 2016 election but that turns out to be remarkable in its anticipation of our current climate: "If [Haidt and others who believe value judgments are more a result of intuition and emotions than of rationality] are right, then we not only have something of an explanation for why knowledge fragmentation continues to persist (people just won't listen to another's reasons) but also a lesson for what to do about it. Or at least what not to do: trying to come up with reasons to convince our cultural opponents isn't going to work."

Many have called for just this—a turning away from logos, away from reason and evidence—to engage (and potentially persuade) political and cultural opponents. In Jess Zimmerman's (2017) aptly titled article "It's Time to Give Up on Facts," she encourages liberals to "lay down their facts and pick up a more useful weapon—emotions." "Engaging on the plane of belief, where lies live," writes Zimmerman (2017), "means taking a break from trying to prove what's factually accurate and talking instead about what feels meaningful in the heart." She explains further:

This doesn't always need to mean letting egregious errors stand—it's worth holding on to the fact that reality exists beyond opinions. But it might well mean breezing past the correction into whatever's keeping the lie alive. Figuring out how to counter falsehoods is going to mean assessing how lies benefit the people telling them. Do the things they believe without evidence make them feel safe? Do they make them feel moral? Do these beliefs contribute to a sense of being superior and unassailable? At the one-on-one level, figuring that out is going to help you more than issuing a verbal correction. (Zimmerman 2017)

How might this approach be relevant as we construct our response to our current post-truth culture? While Zimmerman is not altogether rejecting reason and evidence and neither am I, we can and should expand our own understandings of how people are persuaded and—by extension—our students' understanding of this phenomenon. Our teaching must better reflect the complexities associated with persuasion that are largely neglected in our field. Recognizing ourselves and teaching our students in more comprehensive ways how persuasion works is essential in a climate marked by post-truth discourse.

At the most basic level of definition, then, complications begin to emerge in how the field of rhetoric and composition defines (rational) beliefs and emotion—or, in rhetorical terms, logos and pathos. In her blog *How the Teaching of Rhetoric Has Made Trump Possible*, professor, writing center director, and blogger Patricia Roberts Miller (2016; brackets in the original) describes how our culture's wrong-headed ideas about emotion and rationality seep into our educational systems:

As a culture, we oppose emotion and "rationality," and that means that, to determine if an argument is "rational," we try to infer whether the rhetor is "rational." And we generally do that by trying to infer if the rhetor is letting his/her emotions "distort" their thinking. Or, connected, we rely on a definition of "logic" that is commonly in textbooks—a "logical" argument is one that appeals to facts, statistics, and data. [Notice that an argument might be logical in that sense—it makes those appeals—but completely illogical in the sense of its reasoning (what Aristotle actually meant by "logos").]

As Miller points out, we too often uncritically separate out logos from pathos. Perhaps we have done so by asking our students how someone's (emotional) biases are potentially distorting their thinking. Maybe we've even asked our students how their own biases might distort their thinking. Another challenge that emerges, then, as we consider resisting and responding to the current climate, is our field's oversimplification of the relationship between thought and emotion, between logos and pathos. If "we, as a community of scholars and teachers," are going to "'double down' on the tools we have to combat post truth rhetoric" (McComiskey 2017:38), we had better be working from more complex understandings of the varied relationships between these mental processes. Ultimately, working from these more complex understandings is also a necessary foundation for the kind of empathic reading described in chapter 3, as well as the more general acceptance of the role emotion must play in our teaching and research, as detailed throughout this book.

2. AS A FIELD WE PRIVILEGE ARGUMENTATION

For all the permutations of first-year composition across the country, the course that represents the field of rhetoric and composition in the postsecondary curriculum is most often a course in argumentation, a point Duffy (2012) has not only made but celebrated: "The first-year writing course represents one of the few places in the academic curriculum, in some institutions the only place, where students learn the basics of argument, or how to make a claim, provide evidence, and consider alternative points of view. Argument is the currency of academic discourse, and learning to argue is a necessary skill if students are to succeed in their college careers." As Duffy suggests, learning how to develop sound arguments helps prepare students to succeed in and beyond school. Unfortunately, though, as a field we are beholden to largely impoverished models of argumentation that circulate widely within secondary and postsecondary institutions (Beaufort 2007; Melzer 2014; Sullivan 2014). Patrick Sullivan (2014:12) connects simplistic argumentative essay assignments to the findings from the National Commission on Writing that describe the writing of twelfth graders as "relatively immature and unsophisticated." Drawing on the scholarship of Milka Mustenikova Mosely (2006), Sullivan also points out that workload issues at the secondary level are one of the reasons why the simplistic argumentative essay continues to be taught. I would add that the same reason accounts for its presence in first-year writing courses, many of which are taught by over-worked and underpaid adjuncts. Simply put, simplistic argu-mentative essays are relatively easy to teach and easy to grade, which is important when one is traveling to half a dozen schools on a daily basis.

As a field we need to find a place for modes of argumentation that do not simply mirror the current rhetorical climate, which has only exacerbated what Deborah Tannen (1998) has called our "argument culture." Many in the field of rhetoric and com-position have already sought to (re)define argument as a mode of understanding, collaboration, and negotiation (Frey 1990; Meyer 1993; Salvatori 1996; Brent 1992; Qualley 1997; Sullivan 2014; Miller 2016). The collection *Argument Revisited, Argument Redefined* (Emmel, Resch, and Tenney 1996) strives to redefine and connect argument to key concepts in rhetoric and composi-tion, but as Jennifer L. Bay (2002:687) points out, this work may be more an exercise in theorizing than an effective way of bring-ing about real change in how argumentation is taught: "Because we now value cultural concepts like community, collaboration, and understanding, argument is often refigured to fit those cul-tural goals. Yet while the definition of argument has changed, the process and procedures by which argument is taught remain the same." Bay (2002:687) cites Jeanne Fahnestock and Marie Secor's chapter from *Argument Revisited, Argument Redefined* as evidence of this, specifically their admission that "only classical rhetoric offers a complete, general art of argumentation that takes in the whole activity of discourse making, from the first stages of inquiry to the final stages of dissemination." In other words, Bay reads this invocation of classical rhetoric as an indi-cation that the methods of teaching argumentation have not changed that much despite the contemporary adaptations of the reasons for teaching it. These ways of teaching argument certainly impact not just how our students write arguments but also how they read all kinds of texts, as explored in chapter 3. As such, revisiting how argument is defined and taught in rhetoric and composition has implications for students' development of critical reading habits.

I would posit that one of the reasons the teaching of argumentation has not changed that much over the decades, despite pushes by many in that direction, is that our understanding of argument remains largely grounded in the field of rhetoric and composition. Unfortunately, disciplinary divides make it difficult to approach subjects of study in more comprehensive ways that would allow us to see the teaching of argumentation (and teaching more generally) from different perspectives. For example, the fields of education and psychology (among other fields like biology and neuroscience) have produced research that is germane to literacy instruction, yet so much of this remains unknown by those in rhetoric and composition, including myself. Certainly, rhetoric and composition's recent focus on the transfer of learning and its ongoing interest in motivation have highlighted the importance of bringing educational psychology into our discussions, but largely those in the field of rhetoric and composition do not regularly seek out or have opportunities to regularly review research in other fields. Although rhetoric and composition has long prided itself on its interdisciplinarity and is far more interdisciplinary than many other fields, I don't think rhetoric and composition has gone far enough in exploring what cognitive and educational psychology, for example, might teach us about teaching and learning. The field's understanding of certain phenomenon—as we are currently seeing with the transfer of learning—can be significantly enriched by working across these disciplinary boundaries.

Patrick Sullivan's (2014) "pedagogy of listening" is one such pedagogy that incorporates research and scholarship from beyond rhetoric and composition. This pedagogy draws on ideas related to "learning theory, critical thinking, transfer of knowledge, neuroscience, motivation, cognitive psychology, and characterological dispositions" (Sullivan 2014:180). Sullivan's pedagogical approach suggests an alternative to teaching argumentation as opposition. Instead, he engages students in more collaborative, dialogic, and reflective academic work. What separates Sullivan's approach, though, from those that Bay (2002:687) would call mere "retooling[s] of argument as persuasion for the postmodern world" is its more comprehensive approach, characterized by its reliance on research not just from rhetoric and composition but from many fields with different epistemologies. A large part of this pedagogy involves "reducing our overreliance on argumentative writing, especially simplistic argumentative writing" and making "listening, empathy, and reflection the primary skills we value in our classrooms" (Sullivan 2014:5). Exploratory writing assignments rather than simplistic argument-driven assignments that seek to merely oppose or even annihilate "the other" (Sullivan 2014:105) support this pedagogy.

Sullivan's (2014) rich and comprehensive rendering of this pedagogy that calls into question our field's reliance on argumentation (and, more crucially, simplistic definitions of argumentation) provides a model of how we can do better and why we must do better. Drawing on research from educational and cognitive psychology, Sullivan (2014:59) explains that prompts and courses that depend on simplistic views of argument "actively entren[ch] or tra[p] students at this cognitive stage. There are no opportunities provided for students to move beyond the conceptual boundaries, frontiers, and cognitive limitations of this position." Sullivan (2014:60) explains that what is missing might be described as "listening"—"that is to say, an open, collaborative, dialogical engagement with others," which "is often actively hindered by this pedagogy and kind of writing assignment." Moreover, Sullivan (2014:60) laments that "opportunities to read for nuance and subtlety and to listen carefully to writers they [students] are reading and to fellow classmates in class discussions . . . are often compromised." Notice that simplistic argument-driven prompts, as Sullivan describes them, not only foreclose more complex methods of writing but also compromise reading opportunities. Recognizing the effects of these prompts on reading, as does Sullivan (2014:44), reminds us of the importance of using the classroom to foster not just more complex writing habits but "more humane kinds of reading."

As early as the 1980s, Jim W. Corder was also interested in more humane kinds of reading, writing, and thinking. With the emphasis in the 1970s on Rogerian argument, which Corder (1985:25–26) critiqued on the basis that it was more conducive to therapy than to writing pedagogy, he maintained that we need to "chang[e] the way we talk about argument" by imagining argument as more than simply "display and presentation" wherein we "present a proposition. We display our proofs, our evidence. We show that we can handle and if need be refute opposing views." Corder reads Rogerian argument as adopted by Hairston and others as further exercises in display and presentation. Corder (1985:26) instead says we must learn that "argument is emergence toward the other" that "requires a readiness to testify to an identity that is always emerging, a willingness to dramatize one's narrative in progress before the others; it calls for an untiring stretch toward the other, a reach toward enfolding the other."

The contrast between the kinds of pedagogy Sullivan and Corder describe and the sort of argumentative culture that is so pervasive today is striking. The former describes productive ways of listening and responding to others, and with its emphasis on listening, empathy, compassion, and reflection it incorporates attention to the often overlooked emotional components that are so integral to one's reading, writing, and thinking practices.

Because one's beliefs are inextricably connected to one's emotions (as described by the review of some psychological research above, as well as in chapter 3), to help our students become more reflective readers and writers, we need to give them opportunities to reflect not just on their ideas or beliefs but on those emotions as well, as detailed in chapter 3. Doug Brent (1992:116) has described how one might push past logos to incorporate more attention to emotion in a writing classroom: "To apprehend fully the process of logos, students must work toward discovering how their own doxai allow them to evaluate a work at the same time that the work is persuading them to modify their own doxai . . . By comparing each others' judgments, students can work toward understanding how their own doxai affect their own judgments . . . students must also understand how they can use their emotional as well as their rational reactions to sources." Brent's (1992:116) goal is to help students "avoid being overwhelmed by powerful and immediate emotional judgments . . . [and] also learn not to expel emotional reactions from the process of judgment." In other words, Brent is calling on students to reflect on their own ideas, assumptions, and emotions as they engage with—and listen to—each other. Both Brent and Sullivan, as addressed above, have outlined ways they have found to get beyond logos and the field's dependence on more narrow conceptions of argumentation in favor of more dialogic-based approaches to teaching reading, writing, and thinking.

One can't help but wonder, though, if dialogue is even possible in a post-truth culture, since "the facts" cannot even be agreed upon. Psychology can help here, too, and in the following section, which points out some of the gaps in rhetoric and composition's knowledge base, I explore how as a field we might teach our students about the concept of framing, a tool that has the capacity to inspire and support genuine dialogue.

3. AS A FIELD, WE PRIVILEGE OUR OWN SCHOLARSHIP OVER THAT FROM OTHER FIELDS

It is not particularly surprising that the field of rhetoric and composition privileges its own scholarship over that of other fields. This characterization would likely apply to all fields of study. But remaining within the narrow confines of rhetoric and composition has some significant drawbacks when dealing with a subject like literacy instruction that is studied by many other fields, including education, psychology, neurology, and biology.

Psychology (educational, cognitive, and behavioral) in particular has much to offer rhetoric and composition. Despite the field's foundational connections to the field of psychology, rhetoric and composition largely turned away from psychology fairly early on as it began considering more socially and politically inflected issues. There is important research and scholarship, though, that should be recovered from that period wherein scholars like Ann E. Berthoff (1981a, 1981b) and James Moffett (1968), among others, wrote compellingly about the need to explore the composition of meaning as an embodied practice.

As laid out above, the field of psychology has studied how rationality and belief systems are affected by and inextricably linked to our emotions. As such, the field of psychology can help us think about the psychological dimension of composing meaning, of reading. This does not mean that as a field we have to abandon our investment in logos, in the rational. Instead, we can use research from psychology and related fields to help us understand—and therefore teach—ways to engage in genuine productive dialogue wherein we listen to others and they listen to us.

Informed by psychological research, the aptly named FrameWorks Institute, a communications think tank in Washington, DC, studies "how nonprofit organizations can frame messages to communicate effectively with the public" (Kendall-Taylor 2017). The organization has undertaken extensive research on messaging and how messages can be framed to change beliefs and attitudes. Nat Kendall-Taylor (2017), CEO of the FrameWorks Institute, explains: "Our research shows that facts do matter and that they do have persuasive power—but only if they are well framed." In its studies of how to frame issues like immigration, criminal justice, and child abuse, the institute found that "facts that advocates typically use to educate the public did not change people's opinions" and often "increased negative attitudes toward these issues no matter the person's place on the political spectrum" (Kendall-Taylor 2017). When framed in more pragmatic terms, however, including "robust discussions of solutions," facts "boosted engagement and support for evidence-based programs and policies" (Kendall-Taylor 2017).

With its mixed-methods approach to research that includes—but is not limited to—peer discourse analysis, content analysis, experimental surveys, and what its researchers call Persistence Trials that allow them to evaluate which framing methods "are most easily understood by the public," the FrameWorks Institute is doing the work Zimmerman calls for in "It's Time to Give Up on Facts," described above. The FrameWorks Institute has concluded that simply offering more facts will not lead people to reassess or change their beliefs, a conclusion supported by extensive and foundational scientific research (Ross, Lepper, and Hubbard 1975; Jennings, Lepper, and Ross 1981; Lau 1986; Lord, Ross, and Lepper 1979:). "The mere availability of contradictory evidence rarely seems sufficient to cause us to abandon our prior beliefs or theories," write Charles G. Lord, Lee Ross, and Mark R. Lepper (1979:2108). Instead, the FrameWorks Institute is researching and finding ways—including methods of framing messages—that will get people to engage rather than just outright reject ideas.

Scientists are realizing the value in these framing techniques. In Virginia Gewin's (2017:426) article about how post-truth rhetoric affects science, associate professor of sustainability science at Duke University Xavier Basurto explains:

> If you come from an angle of "science is the truth—you just don't understand the facts," people will not be willing to listen to you. They will find that angle offensive. You need to speak in such a way that people are willing to listen. To do that, it's important to acknowledge that there are many ways of knowing or learning. Humans are not rational, yet we tend to portray ourselves as much more rational than we are. The US election results were surprising because many didn't see them as rational. Incorporating social science into physical and biological sciences is one way to bridge divides in understanding between scientists and non-scientists.

As Basurto points out, recognizing and using the different epistemologies to which people subscribe in order to engage them can be a powerful tool. Framing techniques, like those described above, can be used in the classroom to help our students engage in dialogue across ideological and cultural divides. It gives students an important tool to do so without totally neglecting rational and evidence-based discussions. Rather than simply summoning facts and evidence and assuming they will speak for themselves, students can engage in discussions about the best ways to frame those facts and evidence in their writing and in their encounters with others. Framing may even be a particularly useful pedagogical tool when faced with students who are reluctant to engage multiple perspectives on a topic or read against the grain, two common practices taught in first-year writing courses. In other words, instructors can use framing to help students engage in critical reading practices they otherwise may reject. Beyond potentially providing access to that reluctant student, though, reading the literature in psychology has helped me develop an understanding of the importance of recognizing the magnitude of what we are asking *all* students to do when we expect them to undertake the intellectual work of critical reading. What I have learned about this from psychology, detailed below, has left me surprised that I don't encounter even more reluctant students.

Like Sullivan, whose pedagogy is described above, I encourage students to be reflective readers, thinkers, and writers as well as committed listeners and collaborators, and I am transparent about why I think these are valuable behaviors and enterprises. I largely expect that students will be willing participants in the range of activities I have created to help foster these values, which represent some of the key principles of the field of rhetoric and composition as well as the academy more generally. But our country's divisiveness—and the psychological theories that help explain it (Konnikova 2016)—has resulted in my asking questions about the psychological implications of the underlying values that inform the intellectual work I ask my students to undertake on a regular basis. For example, what are the psychological stakes associated with prompting students to view issues from multiple perspectives, to read against the grain, or to address viewpoints that oppose their own, all of which are critical reading practices? It turns out that when I ask students to undertake this work, I am essentially looking to short-circuit the protections the brain has in place to keep belief systems intact. These protections include psychological phenomena such as cognitive dissonance, confirmation bias, motivated reasoning, and information avoidance, among others. As I read about the role these phenomena likely played in my and others' shock at the 2016 presidential election results (Konnikova 2016), I came to understand a bit more about our country's divisiveness and why it's so hard to overcome. More important, though, from a pedagogical perspective, I have also come to recognize for the first time how the values that undergird the intellectual work I assign students may be psychologically affecting them.

As often as we may make our values visible to our students, I don't think we really understand what, from a psychological perspective, we are asking our students to do when we require them to engage in what we think of as some of the most fundamental intellectual work. When we ask students to explore multiple perspectives, including those that oppose their own, and to read against the grain, we are asking them to reject the very psychological systems that are set up to protect them (all of us) from having to entertain any ideas that do not fit neatly into their worldview. For example, we are trying to short-circuit how confirmation bias and cognitive dissonance protect students and their belief systems. I point this out not to paint us as terrible people but to use these psychological concepts to help our field come to a better understanding of the psychological barriers to the work we routinely expect from our students and to point out how this understanding might inform our response to the current climate.

As noted above, the psychological concepts of confirmation bias and cognitive dissonance are two of the many ways the brain protects itself. Confirmation bias theory describes the tendency to only see evidence that confirms one's position, belief, or idea. Raymond S. Nickerson (1998:176) explains further that "once one has taken a position on an issue, one's primary purpose becomes that of defending or justifying that position. This is to say that regardless of whether one's treatment of evidence was evenhanded before the stand was taken, it can become highly biased afterward." Moreover, he explains that "people tend to seek information that they consider supportive of favored hypotheses or existing beliefs and to interpret information in ways that are partial to those hypotheses or beliefs" (Nickerson 1998:177).

Even when people are not seeking information to support their existing beliefs, the phenomenon of confirmation bias explains how they are able to find confirmation in opposing evidence. Psychologists Charles G. Lord, Lee Ross, and Mark R. Lepper's (1979:2099, emphasis in original) foundational research on the subject demonstrates how "with disconfirming evidence, [people] continue to reflect upon any information that suggests less damaging 'alternative interpretations.' Indeed, they may even come [to] regard the ambiguities and conceptual flaws in the data *opposing* their hypotheses as somehow suggestive of the fundamental *correctness* of those hypotheses." Lord, Ross, and Lepper (1979:2108) ultimately conclude that "in everyday life . . . the mere availability of contradictory evidence rarely seems sufficient to cause us to abandon our prior beliefs or theories."

Just as the theory of confirmation bias describes how someone will only see the evidence that supports her point of view, the theory of cognitive dissonance maintains that "if a person holds two cognitions that are inconsistent with one another, he will experience the pressure of an aversive motivational state called cognitive dissonance, a pressure which he will seek to move, among other ways, by altering one of the two 'dissonant' conditions" (Bem 1967:183). In other words, this person will find a way to compensate for the dissonance so the two opposing cognitions can coexist. The third psychological theory related to these other two cognitions and particularly to cognitive dissonance is motivated reasoning, which explains the impulse to scrutinize ideas more carefully if we don't like them than if we do. Motivated reasoning also "increases the threshold that persuasion attempts need to meet in order to generate a change in positions" (Peterson 2016:1097). From a biological perspective, motivated reasoning may have evolved to "help shield against manipulation" (Peterson 2016:1097). These are significant and well-documented phenomena that affect our students as much as they affect anyone. As such, we need to remind ourselves that the very intellectual work that we expect of our students and that we largely take for granted is work that contradicts our brains' natural responses.

As we look toward deepening our understanding of the psychological barriers we may face as we continue to engage students in this intellectual work—in the sort of critical reading I am describing—it is also worth exploring the lesser-known psychological phenomenon of information avoidance. Like the concepts mentioned above, information avoidance has important bearing on our investment in developing projects and assignments that expect students not only to engage with multiple perspectives but to actively seek out those that challenge their ideas. Psychologists Kate Sweeny, Darya Melnyk, Wendi Miller, and James A. Shepperd (2010:341) define information avoidance as "any behavior intended to prevent or delay the acquisition of available but potentially unwanted information. Information avoidance can entail asking someone not to reveal information, physically leaving a situation to avoid learning information, or simply failing to take the necessary steps to reveal the content of information . . . information avoidance may be temporary or permanent. People may avoid information with the intention of learning the information later, or they may decide to avoid the information altogether." Research in the area of information avoidance "shows that people avoid information to the extent that it threatens their desired affect, cognitions, or behaviors" (Howell, Crosier, and Shepperd 2014:103). Findings across populations, including undergraduate students, indicate that people are less inclined to avoid seeking out potentially threatening information if they feel secure in their support systems and "coping resources," such as family members, peers, or other sources of support (Sweeny et al. 2010; Howell, Crosier, and Shepperd 2014).

If we think about the goals of literacy instruction, some of which I have alluded to throughout this chapter but that are codified in our discipline's professional documents such as the *WPA Outcomes Statement for First-Year Composition* (2014) and the *Framework for Success in Postsecondary Writing* (2011), then we can begin to see specific applications of the theory of information avoidance to our own work, particularly in how we might design activities and assignments. As a field, we strive to teach students how to read and write in ways that reflect the values of open-mindedness, flexibility, perseverance, and curiosity, among others. We expect them to address counterarguments and to look at issues from multiple perspectives. Such work often means they must be willing to engage with information that threatens their worldview. Rather than imagining that we are simply teaching students "the moves that matter in academic writing," we can think about this work within the context of theories of information avoidance, as well as the other theories mentioned above. Doing so helps us understand in a deeper (and psychologically inflected) way why students may have such difficulty with this work. Moreover, the research on information avoidance also suggests how we might better support students as they undertake this work. As discussed above, participants in these scientific studies were less likely to avoid information if they had a strong support group. We can create that support in the classroom in the form of peer groups and other collaborative designs.

Elsewhere, including in chapter 3, I have described how Peter Elbow's Doubting and Believing Game can be used to help students engage opposing points of view, which would include information they might be likely to try to avoid. The Doubting and Believing Game can be used as a reading strategy that encourages the reader to play two roles while reading. First, the reader reads a text as though she believes everything the writer says. Then, the reader rereads the text and takes on the role of the doubter. Both ways of reading—reading to believe and reading to doubt—necessitate that students read a text at least twice. Whereas previously I described this as an individual activity, it makes more sense, in light of what I now know about information avoidance from the field of psychology, to make this more of a collaborative enterprise in which students work together in groups (which act as support systems), since this would make students more likely to seek out texts and ideas that "threate[n] their desired affect, cognitions, or behaviors" (Howell, Crosier, and Shepperd 2014:103). The Doubting and Believing Game demands that students *inhabit* perspectives that are not their own. This "continual practice in trying to have other perceptions and experiences," writes Elbow (2008:170–71), "helps people break out of their 'sets' and preoccupations— helps them be less rigid, less prey to conventional, knee-jerk, or idiosyncratic responses." This work fosters an openness in students that has important consequences not just in the classroom but in the world. Still, this can be high-stakes work for students, and psychology explains just how high-stakes it is, particularly if we think of believing in a more emotionally inflected sense, as described in chapter 3. As such, it follows that creating an especially supportive, collaborative space in which students undertake this work is of the utmost importance.

Before students can explore perspectives beyond their own, though, they need to be aware of their own positions. As Ruth A. Goldfine and Deborah Mixson-Brookshire's (2017:56) study of first-year composition students indicates, "Students have a clear sense of their values and often have positions on many of today's issues but generally lack the knowledge and life experience to articulate the reasons for the beliefs they hold." What Goldfine and Mixson-Brookshire found seems to support Haidt's description of the prevalence of moral dumbfounding, described above. The Doubting and Believing Game can mitigate this moral dumbfounding by helping students better understand what they really think and feel about a subject rather than just allowing them to continue to assume what they should think or feel. In the course of applying this strategy, students often also find that their position on a subject does not necessarily lie on either side of a simplistic binary but is the result of an act of negotiation. As McComiskey (2000:76) describes, negotiation, "a far more valuable reading strategy [than agreeing or disagreeing], requires us to establish our own position in the middle ground among competing texts." Unfortunately, as

McComiskey (2000:75) also points out, negotiation "requires that students learn active reading strategies that most are simply unfamiliar with when they enter college."

As I have suggested throughout this section, when we require active critical reading, we need to really contemplate what—psychologically—we are asking of our students and whether this work is ethical. The time is ripe to focus our efforts on helping students become more open-minded and reflective readers, writers, and thinkers since they also need these qualities to participate as citizens in a democracy that depends on open exchange and compromise. Using research from the field of psychology to inflect this work will allow us to develop a more informed response to the current climate and a deeper understanding of the psychological demands we place on our students as we ask them to take intellectual risks in the classroom.

CONCLUDING THOUGHTS

While I would not go so far as to call the few principles I have laid out in this chapter threshold concepts within rhetoric and composition, they function in largely the same way. They make visible the often-invisible principles on which our field is built and, as such, give those of us in the field the opportunity to examine and reflect on them. Recognizing the unique challenges these principles pose is integral to formulating a compelling response to the current climate. Even if we do commit to the work I laid out here, though, we have at least one additional obstacle to surmount, which only came to my attention in the last week of a Writing through Research class. I was discussing with students how to use qualifiers in their writing to avoid oversimplifications and generalizations, as well as to create a space for readers with different perspectives. Specifically, we were talking about ways academics "hedge" in their writing, how they are careful and cautious about their word choices. We talked about using tempering words like "always" and "never," as well as replacing verbs like "is" with "may be" or "seems," as appropriate. Then, seemingly out of nowhere, a few students started talking about

Microsoft Word. They informed me and the rest of the class of a function in the newest version of Microsoft Word that "dislikes" hedging. They explained that phrases like "may be" get underlined by that ubiquitous MS squiggle, which in updated versions of Word is more like a dotted line. My students weren't talking about the spell check or grammar check squiggles but about a new brownish squiggle. They explained further—and I confirmed later that evening—that when the writer clicks on the identified word or words to find out what the problem is, she is told it is a problem of "clarity and conciseness."

MS Word, it seems, does not appreciate qualifiers and encourages students to remove them. The program favors "is" to "may be" and "seems to be." In terms of conciseness, the program has a point. Strunk and White would likely agree. But inasmuch as writing is a form of thinking, Microsoft Word is trying to shut down the more open and dialogic modes of thinking that support the promising pedagogies developed by Duffy, Sullivan, and Brent, as described in this chapter. Essentially, Microsoft Word is doing more than prompting students to value concision; it is prompting them to value certainty and conviction over openness and humility. It is, in Sullivan's (2014:57) words, prompting students to "cultivate an artificial sense of authority and 'mastery.'"

As reflective as we might be on our own field's values, as willing as we may be to find ways to bump logos down a notch, to loosen our grip on simplistic modes of argumentation, to venture into the field of psychology more regularly, the very technologies our students are using to compose are steering them away from the language of negotiation and compromise. Certainly, writing technologies have always necessarily affected the writing they help produce, and this is, of course, a subject of great interest within rhetoric and composition, as well as one that is far beyond the scope of this chapter. Still, I think it is worth keeping in mind that as we teach within this highly divisive post-truth context, there will inevitably be obstacles that seem to target and undermine our very goals, some of which I have outlined in this chapter. We'll need to work together to find ways over and around these obstacles, including that darn Microsoft Word squiggle that has the potential to influence the thinking of the billions of people worldwide who regularly use Microsoft Word.[22]

NOTES

1. For pre- and post-2016 election views on this divisiveness, see Achenbach and Clement (2016); Shapiro (2016); "A Country Divided by Counties" (2016); Pilkington (2017).

2. For a history of fake news stories dating back to the 1800s, see Steven Seidenberg's (2017) "Yesterday's (Fake) News."

3. Although the term *post-truth* was first used in 1992 in an article by Steve Tesich published in *The Nation*, the *Oxford English Dictionary* named "post-truth" the word of the year in 2016. The *OED* also reports a 2,000 percent increase in its use since 2015.

4. See, for example, initial Trump campaign manager Corey Lewandowski's statement to the media (cited in Blake 2016) in which he devalues the importance of facts: "You guys took everything that Donald Trump said so literally . . . The American people didn't. They understood it. They understood that sometimes—when you have a conversation with people . . . you're going to say things, and sometimes you don't have all the facts to back it up." Scottie Nell Hughes, Trump supporter and CNN commentator, remarked similarly (on the Diane Rehm show): "People that say that facts are facts—they're not really facts . . . there's no such thing, unfortunately, anymore of facts. And so Mr. Trump's tweet amongst a certain crowd . . . are truth" (Marcus 2016). Finally, when confronted about the misinformation the White House was spreading, including the number of attendees at Trump's inauguration, Trump's counselor Kellyanne Conway said the administration was working from what she called "alternative facts" (*Meet the Press* 2017).

5. Alice Horning (2007) notes that while critically reading, students should be able to do the following: "They must be able to analyze, including summary of key points, main ideas and the point of view of a writer. They must be able to synthesize, that is, draw ideas together from several sources to support their own views and ideas. And finally, readers should be able to evaluate what they are reading, judging authority, accuracy, relevance, timeliness, and bias."

6. Although I use the (singular) term *response* here and throughout the book, I do not intend to suggest that a single, unified response is necessary.

Instead, I recognize that there will be a range of responses from the field of rhetoric and composition to the current climate, and I encourage individual instructors, WPAs, and others to consider productive responses.

7.   A version of this chapter was previously published as Carillo (2016). © 2016 by the National Council of Teachers of English. Used with permission.

8.   Arthur Applebee (1974:163) describes *Understanding Poetry* as the "single most important influence in transforming such critical theory into classroom practice," and it appeared as one of fifteen books on *The English Journal*'s list of "pre-1950 books about (or on) the English curriculum worth reading today" in Donelson (1984:83).

9.   Although not focused on students, in their study of the spread of true and false news online, MIT researchers Soroush Vosoughi, Deb Roy, and Sinan Aral (2018:1146) found that "contrary to conventional wisdom, robots accelerated the spread of true and false news at the same rate, implying that false news spreads more than the truth because humans, not robots, are more likely to spread it." This large-scale study investigated the "diffusion of all of the verified true and false stories distributed on Twitter from 2006 to 2017," which amounted to approximately "126,000 stories tweeted by approximately 3 million people more than 4.5 million times" (Vosoughi, Roy, and Aral 2018:1146). Ultimately, the researchers conclude that "human behavior contributes more to the differential spread of falsity and truth than automated robots do . . . [and that] understanding how false news spreads is the first step toward containing it" (Vosoughi, Roy, and Aral 2018:1146). Paying attention to emerging studies of how fake news spreads can help educators develop pedagogies informed by these findings.

10. For more on this threat to democracy, see guest editors' Thomas P. Miller and Adele Leon's (2017) special issue of *Literacy in Composition Studies* titled "Literacy, Democracy, and Fake News: Making It Right in the Era of Fast and Slow Literacies."

11. Composition has recently seen a renewed interest in affect, as evidenced by guest editor Lance Langdon's (2016) special issue of *Composition Forum*, on emotion; guest editors' Kathy Evertz and Renata Fitzpatrick's (2018) special issue of *WLN: A Journal of Writing Center Scholarship*, on the affective dimension of writing center work; and the forthcoming collection edited by Courtney Adams Wooten, Jacob Babb, Kristi Murray Costello, and Kate Navickas titled *The Things We Carry: Strategies for Recognizing and Negotiating Emotional Labor in Writing Program Administration*.

12. It is worth at least acknowledging that emotions have long been circumscribed as feminine in Western cultures and associated with weakness. The affective turn builds on feminist critiques of emotion in that scholars including Micciche, Jacobs, and McLeod, among others, explore emotions as socially constructed rather than as biologically bound. Although cognitive psychologists, neurobiologists, philosophers, literary critics, and senators (e.g., Barack Obama discussed empathy at his 2006 commencement address at Northwestern University) have emphasized the

role and importance of empathy (and emotion more broadly) in our daily lives and in a democracy and have acknowledged, as does Suzanne Keen (2007:6), that "empathy seems so basic a human trait that lacking it can be seen as a sign of inhumanity," the field of rhetoric and composition has been hesitant to fully embrace emotionally inflected theories and pedagogies. Moreover, as Dennis Lynch (1998:6) has noted, in rhetorical theory, empathy has been devalued and posited as "weak, epistemologically flawed, and politically suspicious." Perhaps those in the already feminized field of rhetoric and composition worry about the implications of foregrounding emotion because emotion itself is regularly feminized.

13.   For example, over the years, many of my students have criticized Woolf (1957, 2003) for going back on her claims in *A Room of One's Own* and "How Should One Read a Book?" As I (Carillo 2010:381) describe in that article:

> Students point to any number of conclusions that Woolf, in fact, offers throughout *A Room of One's Own*, including her most famous conclusion—that a woman needs money and a room of her own in order to write. Similarly, when Woolf says she refuses to answer the title question in "How Should One Read a Book?" and then goes on to do so, students, such as Courtney, call Woolf "hypocritical" and another student, Liz, labels the disjunction an "oxymoron." Students had similar responses when I taught Kincaid's *A Small Place* and "On Seeing England for the First Time," as well as Sven Birkerts' "Mah-VuhHuhPuh." Maddie spent her essay on Birkerts' piece describing the range of contradictions in it while Massimo, coming from a similar perspective, wrote of Kincaid: "A lot of times she contradicts herself. For example with the 'you' in *A Small Place*."

14.   See Carillo (2015) for more on this.

15.   One place where Elbow (2003:ix) connects methodological believing to emotion is in his foreword to *A Way to Move*: "The believing game invites thinking with feelings (though it doesn't require it) . . . Feelings may not be the main thing about the believing game, but in the context of this book, I want to emphasize how the believing game invites the harnessing of feelings for the sake of better thinking." Readers will notice that Elbow concedes that feelings are not central to his conception of methodological believing, but he describes them as more central than he has elsewhere for the purpose of introducing the book.

16.   This shift has been criticized by some in the field. See, for example, Gross and Alexander (2016) and Belli (2016).

17.   For a discussion of the embarrassment students (and the rest of us) feel upon forgetting what we have read, see pages 120–33 in Newkirk (2017).

18.   Media professor Melissa Zimdars (2016) separates fake news into four broad categories. In the first category, she describes fake news as that which "us[es] distorted headlines and decontextualized or dubious information in order to generate likes, shares, and profits."

19.   While my students and I largely rely on handwritten annotations, I am making the transition to digital annotation platforms in some of my classes. For instructors who might be interested in encouraging digital annotation, there are many options. Students can download an annotation management system like Diigo for free at https://www.diigo .com/. Students may add sticky notes to any webpage with https://www .mystickies.com/ for free. The comment feature in Adobe Reader (available for free download) is also a great resource that allows students to both highlight and comment on texts. Some of these platforms also allow students to share their annotations.

20.   For a compelling account of these "sealed-off worlds," specifically the difference between echo chambers and epistemic bubbles, see Nguyen (2018).

21.   Haidt is not without detractors. Yale psychologist Paul Bloom (2014), for example, believes that "the existence of moral dumbfounding is less damning than it might seem. It is not the rule. People are not at a loss when asked why drunk driving is wrong, or why a company shouldn't pay a woman less than a man for the same job, or why you should hold the door open for someone on crutches. We can easily justify these views by referring to fundamental concerns about harm, equity, and kindness." Moreover, Bloom (2014) points out, "If our moral attitudes are entirely the result of nonrational factors, such as gut feelings and the absorption of cultural norms, they should either be stable or randomly drift over time, like skirt lengths or the widths of ties. They shouldn't show systematic change over human history."

22.   In 2016 Microsoft reported that 1.2 billon people worldwide use Microsoft Office, which includes Microsoft Word in its suite of programs and services (Microsoft n.d.). High-tech strategic services and specialized tech research firm Creative Strategies recently conducted a study of 1,200 students at forty-four colleges across the country (Ben Bajarin, personal email correspondence, August 2, 2017). Matt Richman (2016) reports that 80 percent of students use Microsoft Word for individual work and 13 percent use it for group work. Moreover, "The dynamic is the same for all millennials, regardless of gender, the phone they use, or where they live" (Richman 2016). Richman (2016) explains further, "Not even losing important files in a computer crash prompts millennials to start using Google Docs for individual work, even though doing so would prevent future file losses. There is so much behavioral debt [entrenched behavior that accumulates over time] associated with using Microsoft Word for individual work, not even a catastrophic event can overcome it."

REFERENCES

Achenbach, Joel, and Scott Clement. 2016. "America Really Is More Divided Than Ever." *Washington Post*, July 16.

Adler-Kassner, Linda. 2017. "Because Writing Is Never Just Writing." Chair's Address, Conference on College Composition and Communication, Portland, OR. Accessed April 30, 2017. http://adlerkassner.net/CCCCChair/because -writing-is-never-just-writing-cccc-chairs-address/.

Alexander, Jonathan, and Jacqueline Rhodes. 2014. "Flattening Effects: Composition's Multicultural Imperative and the Problem of Narrative Coherence." *College Composition and Communication* 65 (3): 430–54.

Applebee, Arthur N. 1974. *Tradition and Reform in the Teaching of English.* Urbana, IL: National Council of Teachers of English.

Association of American Colleges and Universities. 2007. "College Learning for the New Global Century." https://www.aacu.org/sites/default/files/files /LEAP/GlobalCentury_final.pdf.

Association of American Colleges and Universities. 2009a. "Civic Engagement VALUE Rubric." https://www.aacu.org/value/rubrics/inquiry-analysis.

Association of American Colleges and Universities. 2009b. "Creative Thinking VALUE Rubric." https://www.aacu.org/value/rubrics/inquiry-analysis.

Ballenger, Bruce. 1997. "Skating Backwards on Thin Ice: Teaching the Research Essay." In *Beyond Note Cards: Rethinking the Research Paper*, ed. Bruce Ballenger, 96–130. Portsmouth, NH: Heinemann.

Bartholomae, David. 2016. "The Study of Error." In *Writing on the Margin: Essays on Composition and Teaching*, ed. David Bartholomae, 19–35. New York: Bedford/St. Martins.

Bartholomae, David, and Beth Matway. 2010. "The Pittsburgh Study of Writing." *Across the Disciplines* 7. https://wac.colostate.edu/atd/articles/bartholomae _matway2010/index.cfm.

Bartholomae, David, and Anthony Petrosky. 1986. *Fact, Artifacts, and Counterfacts.* Portsmouth, NH: Boynton/Cook.

Batson, C. Daniel. 2009. "These Things Called Empathy." In *The Social Neuroscience of Empathy*, ed. William Ickes and Jean Decety, 3–16. Cambridge, MA: MIT Press. https://doi.org/10.7551/mitpress/9780262012973.003.0002.

DOI: 10.7330/9781607327912.c006

Bay, Jennifer L. 2002. "The Limits of Argument: A Response to Sean Williams." *Journal of Advanced Composition* 22 (3): 684–97.

Bean, John C. 2011. *Engaging Ideas*, 2nd ed. San Francisco: Jossey-Bass.

Beaufort, Anne. 2007. *College Writing and Beyond*. Logan: Utah State University Press.

Belli, Jill. 2016. "Why Well-Being, Why Now? Tracing an Alternate Genealogy of Emotion in Composition." *Composition Forum* 34. http://compositionforum .com/issue/34/why-well-being.php.

Bem, Daryl J. 1967. "Self Perception: An Alternative Interpretation of Cognitive Dissonance Phenomena." *Psychological Review* 74 (3): 183–200. https://doi .org/10.1037/h0024835.

Berthoff, Ann E. 1981a. *Forming/Thinking/Writing*. Montclair, NJ: Boynton/ Cook.

Berthoff, Ann E. 1981b. *The Making of Meaning*. Montclair, NJ: Boynton/Cook.

Birkerts, Sven. 1994. "MahVuhHuhPuh." In *The Gutenberg Elegies*, 11–32. New York: Farrar, Strauss, and Giroux.

Bizzell, Patricia. 2000. "Feminist Methods of Research in the History of Rhetoric: What Difference Do They Make?" *Rhetoric Society Quarterly* 30 (4): 5–17. https://doi.org/10.1080/02773940009391186.

Blake, Aaron. 2016. "Corey Lewandowski's Very Odd Explanation of Donald Trump's 'Facts.'" *Washington Post*, December 2. https://www.washingtonpost. com/news/the-fix/wp/2016/12/02/corey-lewandowskis-very-odd-explana tion-of-donald-trumps-facts/?noredirect=on&utm_term=.950b499a3365.

Blau, Sheridan. 2003a. *The Literature Workshop: Teaching Texts and Their Readers*. New York: Heinemann.

Blau, Sheridan. 2003b. "Performative Literacy: The Habits of Mind of Highly Literate Readers." *Voices from the Middle* 10 (3): 18–22.

Blau, Sheridan. 2014. "Literary Competence and the Experience of Literature." *Style* 48: 42–47.

Bloom, Paul. 2014. "The War on Reason." *Atlantic* (Boston), March. https://www .theatlantic.com/magazine/archive/2014/03/the-war-on-reason/357561/.

Bourelle, Andrew. 2009. "Lessons from Quintilian: Writing and Rhetoric across the Curriculum for the Modern University." *Currents in Teaching and Learning* 1 (2): 28–36.

Brent, Doug. 1992. *Reading as Rhetorical Invention*. Urbana, IL: National Council of Teachers of English.

Brooks, Cleanth. 1945. "Letter to Robert Penn Warren." Robert Penn Warren Papers. Box 202, Folder 3569, Beinecke Rare Book and Manuscript Collection. Yale University, New Haven, CT.

Brooks, Cleanth, and Robert Penn Warren. 1938. *Understanding Poetry*. New York: Henry Holt.

Brooks, Cleanth, and Robert Penn Warren. 1950. *Understanding Poetry*, 2nd ed. New York: Henry Holt.

Bunn, Michael. 2013. "Motivation and Connection: Teaching Reading (and Writing) in the Composition Classroom." *College Composition and Communication* 64: 496–516.

Butler, Paul. 2008. *Out of Style: Reanimating Stylistic Study in Composition and Rhetoric*. Logan: Utah State University Press.

Cadwalladr, Carole. 2017. "Daniel Dennett: 'I Begrudge Every Hour I Have to Spend Worrying about Politics.' " Interview with Daniel Dennett. *The Guardian*, February 12. https://www.theguardian.com/science/2017/feb/12/daniel-dennett-politics-bacteria-bach-back-dawkins-trump-interview.

Carillo, Ellen C. 2010. "(Re)figuring Composition through Stylistic Study." *Rhetoric Review* 29 (4): 379–94. https://doi.org/10.1080/07350198.2010.510061.

Carillo, Ellen C. 2015. *Securing a Place for Reading in Composition: The Importance of Teaching for Transfer.* Logan: Utah State University Press.

Carillo, Ellen C. 2016. "Reconnecting the Reader and the Text: Reimagining the Role of the Reader in the Common Core State Standards." *English Journal* 105 (3): 29–35.

Carillo, Ellen C. 2017a. "How Students Read: Some Thoughts on Why This Matters." *English Journal* 106 (5): 34–39.

Carillo, Ellen C. 2017b. "A Place for Reading in the *Framework for Success in Postsecondary Writing*: Recontextualizing the Habits of Mind." In *The Framework for Success in Postsecondary Writing: Scholarship and Applications*, ed. Nicholas Behm, Sherry Rankins-Robertson, and Duane Roen, 38–53. Anderson, SC: Parlor.

Charney, Davida. 1996. "Empiricism Is Not a Four-Letter Word." *College Composition and Communication* 47 (4): 567–93.

Cillizza, Chris. 2015. "How Annotation Can Save Journalism." *Washington Post*, October 7. https://www.washingtonpost.com/news/the-fix/wp/2015/10/07/why-i-believe-annotation-is-the-future-of-journalism/?utm_term=.a4cac7053d6d.

Cioffi, Frank L. 2005. *The Imaginative Argument: A Practical Manifesto for Writers.* Princeton, NJ: Princeton University Press.

Clark, Ruth. 2008. *Building Expertise: Cognitive Methods for Training and Performance Improvement*, 3rd ed. San Francisco: John Wiley and Sons.

Clore, Gerald L., and Karen Gasper. 2000. "Feeling Is Believing: Some Affective Influences on Belief." In *Emotions and Beliefs: How Feelings Influence Thoughts*, ed. Nico H. Frijda, Anthony S.R. Manstead, and Sacha Bem, 10–36. Cambridge: Cambridge University Press.

Cody, Jim. 1996. "The Importance of Expressive Language in Preparing Basic Writers for College Writing." *Journal of Basic Writing* 15 (2): 95–111.

Coleman, David. 2011. "Bringing the Common Core to Life." Keynote Address. New York State Department of Education. Chancellors Hall, State Education Building, Albany, NY, April 28.

Coleman, David, and Susan Pimentel. 2012. *Revised Publishers' Criteria for the Common Core State Standards in English Language Arts and Literacy, Grades 3–12.* www.corestandards.org/assets/Publishers_Criteria_for_3-12.pdf.

Collins, Billy. 1996. "Marginalia." https://www.poetryfoundation.org/poetrymagazine/browse?contentId=39493.

Connors, Robert. 2000. "The Erasure of the Sentence." *College Composition and Communication* 52 (1): 96–128.

Coplan, Amy. 2011. "Understanding Empathy: Its Features and Effects." In *Empathy: Philosophical and Psychological Perspectives*, ed. Amy Coplan and Peter Goldie, 3–18. New York: Oxford University Press. https://doi.org/10.1093/acprof:oso/9780199539956.003.0002.

Corder, Jim W. 1985. "Argument as Emergence, Rhetoric as Love." *Rhetoric Review* 4 (1): 16–32. https://doi.org/10.1080/07350198509359100.

Coughlin, Sean. 2017. "What Does Post-Truth Mean for a Philosopher?" *BBC*, January 12. http://www.bbc.com/news/education-38557838.

"A Country Divided by Counties." 2016. The *Economist*. https://www.economist.com/blogs/graphicdetail/2016/11/daily-chart-7.

D'Ancona, Matthew. 2017. *Post-Truth: The New War on Truth and How to Fight Back.* London: Penguin.

Decety, Jean. 2010. "The Neurodevelopment of Empathy in Humans." *Developmental Neuroscience* 32 (4): 257–67. https://doi.org/10.1159/000317771.

DeStigter, Todd. 1999. "Public Displays of Affection: Political Community through Critical Empathy." *Research in the Teaching of English* 33 (3): 235–44.

Donelson, Ken. 1984. "Books from the Past for the Present." *English Journal* 73 (3): 83. https://doi.org/10.2307/817231.

Driscoll, Dana, and Jennifer Wells. 2012. "Beyond Knowledge and Skills: Writing Transfer and the Role of Student Dispositions." *Composition Forum* 26. http://compositionforum.com/issue/26/.

Duffy, John. 2012. "Virtuous Arguments." *InsideHigherEd*, March 16. https://www.insidehighered.com/views/2012/03/16/essay-value-first-year-writing-courses.

Duffy, John. 2017. "Radical Humilities: Post-Truth, Ethics, and the Teaching of Writing." Keynote Address. University of Connecticut's Twelfth Annual Conference on the Teaching of Writing, Storrs, CT, April 7.

Duncan, Seth, and Lisa Feldman Barrett. 2007. "Affect Is a Form of Cognition: A Neurobiological Analysis." *Cognition and Emotion* 21 (6):1184–1211. https://doi.org/10.1080/02699930701437931 https://www.ncbi.nlm.nih.gov/pmc/articles/PMC2396787/.

Ede, Lisa. 1984. "Is Rogerian Rhetoric Really Rogerian?" *Rhetoric Review* 3 (1): 40–48. https://doi.org/10.1080/07350198409359078.

Eich, Eric, and Jonathan W. Schooler. 2000. "Cognition/Emotion Interactions." In *Cognition/Emotion*, ed. Eric Eich, John F. Kihlstrom, Gordon H. Bower, Joseph Forgas, and Paula M. Niedenthal, 3–29. New York: Oxford University Press.

Elbow, Peter. 2003. Foreword. In *A Way to Move: Rhetorics of Emotion and Composition Studies*, ed. Dale Jacobs and Laura R. Micciche, vii–xii. Portsmouth, NH: Boynton/Cook.

Elbow, Peter. 2005. "Bringing the Rhetoric of Assent and the Believing Game Together—and into the Classroom." *College English* 67 (4): 388–99. https://doi.org/10.2307/30044680.

Elbow, Peter. 2008. "The Believing Game—Methodological Believing." English Department Faculty Publication Series 5. https://scholarworks.umass.edu/eng_faculty_pubs/5.

Emmel, Barbara, Paula Resch, and Deborah Tenney, eds. 1996. *Argument Revisited, Argument Redefined: Negotiating Meaning in the Composition Classroom.* Thousand Oaks, CA: Sage.

Endacott, Jason, and Christian Z. Goering. 2014. "Reclaiming the Conversation on Education." *English Journal* 103 (5): 89–92.

Evertz, Kathy, and Renata Fitzpatrick, eds. 2018. *WLN: A Journal of Writing Center Scholarship* 42 (9–10) (special issue).

Farmer, Frank M., and Phillip K. Arrington. 1993. "Apologies and Accommodations: Imitation and the Writing Process." *Rhetoric Society Quarterly* 23 (1): 2–34.

Ferguson, Daniel E. 2013–14. "Martin Luther King Jr. and the Common Core: A Critical Reading of 'Close' Reading." *Rethinking Schools* 28 (2). https://www.rethinkingschools.org/archive/28_02/28_02_ferguson.shtml.

Flower, Linda. 1990. "Studying Cognition in Context." In *Reading to Write*, ed. Linda Flower, Victoria Stein, John Ackerman, Margaret J. Kantz, Kathleen McCormick, and Wayne C. Peck, 3–32. New York: Oxford University Press.

Framework for Success in Postsecondary Writing. 2011. Council of Writing Program Administrators. http://wpacouncil.org/framework.

Frey, Olivia. 1990. "Beyond Literary Darwinism: Women's Voices and Critical Discourse." *College English* 52 (5): 507–26. https://doi.org/10.2307/377539.

Frijda, Nico H., Anthony S.R. Manstead, and Sacha Bem. 2000. *Emotions and Beliefs: How Feelings Influence Thoughts*. Cambridge: Cambridge University Press. https://doi.org/10.1017/CBO9780511659904.

Frijda, Nico H., and Batja Mesquita. 2000. "Beliefs through Emotions." In *Emotions and Beliefs: How Feelings Influence Thoughts*, ed. Nico H. Frijda, Anthony S.R. Manstead, and Sacha Bem, 45–77. Cambridge: Cambridge University Press.

George, Diana. 1999. *Kitchen Cooks, Plate Twirlers, and Troubadours: Writing Program Administrators Tell Their Stories*. Portsmouth, NH: Heinemann.

Gewertz, Catherine. 2016. "Which States Are Using PARCC or Smarter Balanced?" *Education Week*, February 15. https://www.edweek.org/ew/section/multimedia/states-using-parcc-or-smarter-balanced.html.

Gewin, Virginia. 2017. "Communication: Post-Truth Predicaments." *Nature* 541 (7637): 425–27. https://doi.org/10.1038/nj7637-425a.

Gilbert, Chris. 2014. "A Call for Subterfuge: Shielding the ELA Classroom from the Restrictive Sway of the Common Core." *English Journal* 104 (2): 27–33.

Goldfine, Ruth A., and Deborah Mixson-Brookshire. 2017. "Influence of the College Composition Classroom on Students' Values and Beliefs." In *Writing Pathways to Student Success*, ed. Lillian Craton, Renée Love, and Sean Barnette, 49–58. WAC Clearinghouse. https://wac.colostate.edu/books/pathways/chapter6.pdf.

Golding, Alan. 1995. *From Outlaw to Classic: Canons in American Poetry*. Madison: University of Wisconsin Press.

Goldschmidt, Mary. 2010. "Marginalia: Teaching Texts, Teaching Readers, Teaching Writers." *Reader* 60: 51–69.

Graff, Gerald, and Cathy Birkenstein. 2015. *They Say/I Say: The Moves That Matter in Academic Writing*, 3rd ed. New York: Norton.

Gross, Daniel M., and Jonathan Alexander. 2016. "Frameworks for Failure, Or What Happened to the Social Turn in Writing Studies?" *Pedagogy* 16 (2): 273–95. https://doi.org/10.1215/15314200-3435884.

Haas, Christina, and Linda Flower. 1988. "Rhetorical Reading Strategies and the Construction of Meaning." *College Composition and Communication* 39 (2): 167–83. https://doi.org/10.2307/358026.

Haidt, Jonathan. 2001. "The Emotional Dog and Its Rational Tail: A Social Intuitionist Approach to Moral Judgment." *Psychological Review* 108: 814–34.

Hairston, Maxine. 1976. "Carl Rogers' Alternative to Traditional Rhetoric." *College Composition and Communication* 27 (4): 373–77. https://doi.org/10.2307 /356300.

Harkin, Patricia. 2005. "The Reception of Reader-Response Theory." *College Composition and Communication* 56 (3): 410–25.

Hartman, Saidiya V. 1997. *Scenes of Subjection: Terror, Slavery, and Self-Making in Nineteenth-Century America.* New York: Oxford University Press.

Haswell, Richard H. 1988. "Error and Change in College Student Writing." *Written Communication* 5 (4): 479–99. https://doi.org/10.1177/074108838 8005004005.

Haswell, Richard H. 2005. "NCTE/CCCC's Recent War on Scholarship." *Written Communication* 22 (2): 198–223.

Hein, Grit, and Tania Singer. 2008. "I Feel How You Feel but Not Always: The Empathic Brain and Its Modulation." *Current Opinion in Neurobiology* 18 (2): 153–58. https://doi.org/10.1016/j.conb.2008.07.012.

Heyboer, Kelly. 2015. "PARCC Exams: How Pearson Landed the Deal to Produce N.J.'s Biggest Test." NJ.Com. http://www.nj.com/education/2015/03/parcc _exams_how_pearson_landed_the_deal_to_produce.html.

Hjortshoj, Keith. 2009. *The Transition to College Writing.* 2nd ed. New York: Bedford/St. Martin's.

Holt, Mara. 1999. "On Coming to Voice." In *Kitchen Cooks, Plate Twirlers, and Troubadours,* ed. Diana George, 26–43. Portsmouth, NH: Boynton/Cook.

Horning, Alice S. 2007. "Reading across the Curriculum as the Key to Student Success." *Across the Disciplines* 4. https://wac.colostate.edu/atd/articles/horn ing2007.cfm.

Horning, Alice S. 2011. "Where to Put the Manicules: A Theory of Expert Reading." *Across the Disciplines* 8 (2). https://wac.colostate.edu/atd/articles/horning 2011/index.cfm.

Horning, Alice S. 2012. *Reading, Writing, and Digitizing Literacy in the Electronic Age.* Newcastle upon Tyne, GB: Cambridge Scholars Publishing.

Horning, Alice. 2014. "What Is College Reading? A College-High School Dialogue." *Reader* 67: 43–72.

Horning, Alice S. 2017a. "Enhancing the Framework for Success: Adding Experiences in Critical Reading." In *The Framework for Success in Postsecondary Writing: Scholarship and Applications,* ed. Nicholas Behm, Sherry Rankins-Robertson, and Duane Roen, 54–68. Anderson, SC: Parlor.

Horning, Alice S. 2017b. "Reading: Securing Its Place in the Writing Center." *WLN: A Journal of Writing Center Scholarship* 41 (7–8): 2–8.

Horning, Alice S., Deborah-Lee Gollnitz, and Cynthia Haller, eds. 2017. *What Is College Reading?* Fort Collins, Colorado: The WAC Clearinghouse and University Press of Colorado. http://wac.colostate.edu/books/atd/collegereading/.

Howard, Rebecca Moore. 1992. "A Plagiarism Pentimento." *Journal of Teaching Writing* 11 (3): 233–46.

Howard, Rebecca Moore, Tricia Serviss, and Tanya K. Rodrigue. 2010. "Writing from Sources, Writing from Sentences." *Writing and Pedagogy* 2 (2): 177–92. https://doi.org/10.1558/wap.v2i2.177.

Howell, Jennifer L., Benjamin S. Crosier, and James A. Shepperd. 2014. "Does Lacking Threat-Management Resources Increase Information Avoidance? A

Multi-Sample, Multi-Method Investigation." *Journal of Research in Personality* 50: 102–9. https://doi.org/10.1016/j.jrp.2014.03.003.

Hull, Glynda, and Mike Rose. 1989. "Rethinking Remediation: Toward a Social-Cognitive Understanding of Problematic Reading and Writing." *Written Communication* 6 (2): 139–54. https://doi.org/10.1177/0741088389006002001.

Hull, Glynda, and Mike Rose. 1990. " 'This Wooden Shack Place': The Logic of an Unconventional Reading." In *The Braddock Essays: 1975–1988,* ed. Lisa Ede, 272–82. New York: Bedford/St. Martins.

Iser, Wolfgang. 1978. *The Act of Reading: A Theory of Aesthetic Response.* Baltimore: Johns Hopkins University Press.

Jacobs, Dale, and Laura R. Micciche. 2003. *A Way to Move: Rhetorics of Emotion and Composition Studies.* Portsmouth, NH: Boynton/Cook.

Jaggar, Alison M. 1989. "Love and Knowledge: Emotion in Feminist Epistemology." In *Gender/Body/Knowledge: Feminist Reconstructions of Being and Knowing,* ed. Alison M. Jaggar and Susan R. Bordo, 151–71. New Brunswick, NJ: Rutgers University Press. https://doi.org/10.1080/00201748908602185.

Jamieson, Sandra. 2013. "Reading and Engaging Sources: What Students' Use of Sources Reveals about Advanced Reading Skills." *Across the Disciplines* 10 (4). https://wac.colostate.edu/atd/reading/index.cfm.

Jennings, Dennis L., Mark R. Lepper, and Lee Ross. 1981. *Personality and Social Psychology Bulletin* 7 (2): 257–63.

Jochim, Ashley, and Patrick McGuinn. 2016. "The Politics of the Common Core Assessments." *Education Next* 16 (4): 45–52. http://educationnext.org/the-politics-of-common-core-assessments-parcc-smarter-balanced/.

Johnson, Dan R. 2012. "Transportation into Story Increases Empathy, Prosocial Behavior, and Perceptual Bias toward Fearful Expressions." *Personality and Individual Differences* 52 (2): 150–55. https://doi.org/10.1016/j.paid.2011.10.005.

Jolliffe, David A., and Allison Harl. 2008. "Studying the 'Reading Transition' from High School to College: What Are Our Students Reading and Why?" *College English* 70 (6): 599–617.

Jordan, Elise. 2017. "Trump, Annotated." *Time,* January 20. Accessed July 14, 2017. http://time.com/donald-trump-annotated-inaugural-speech/.

Kearney, Julie. 2009. "Rogerian Principles and the Writing Classroom: A History of Intention and (Mis)Interpretation." *Rhetoric Review* 28 (2): 167–84. https://doi.org/10.1080/07350190902740034.

Keen, Suzanne. 2007. *Empathy and the Novel.* Oxford: Oxford University Press.

Kendall-Taylor, Nat. 2017. "The Power of Fact in a 'Post-Truth' World." *Frank,* April 4. Accessed June 12, 2017. http://frank.jou.ufl.edu/2017/04/fact-post-truth-world/.

Kidd, David Comer, and Emanuel Castano. 2013. "Reading Literary Fiction Improves Theory of Mind." *Science* 342 (6156): 377–80. https://doi.org/10.1126/science.1239918.

Kincaid, Jamaica. 1988. *A Small Place.* New York: Farrar, Strauss, and Giroux.

Kitzhaber, Albert R. 1963. *Themes, Theories, and Therapy: The Teaching of Writing in College.* New York: McGraw-Hill.

Konnikova, Maria. 2016. "The Psychological Research That Helps Explain the Election." *New Yorker,* December 26. Accessed July 1, 2017. https://www.new

yorker.com/science/maria-konnikova/the-psychological-research-that-helps
-explain-the-election.

Langdon, Lance, ed. 2016. *Composition Forum* 34 (special issue). http://compo
sitionforum.com/issue/34/.

Lau, Richard R. 1986. "Persistence of Inaccurate Beliefs about the Self: Perseverance Effects in the Classroom." *Journal of Personality and Social Psychology*
50 (3): 482–91.

Law, Louise. 2016. "PARCC Is Out of Line." Edcircuit. http://www.edcircuit.com
/parcc-the-good-bad-the-ugly/.

Leake, Eric. 2016. "Writing Pedagogies of Empathy: As Rhetoric and Disposition."
Composition Forum 34. http://compositionforum.com/issue/34.

Lindhé, Anna. 2016. "The Paradox of Narrative Empathy and the Form of the
Novel, or What George Eliot Knew." *Studies in the Novel* 48 (1): 19–42. https:/
/doi.org/10.1353/sdn.2016.0011.

Lord, Charles G., Lee Ross, and Mark R. Lepper. 1979. "Biased Assimilation and
Attitude Polarization: The Effects of Prior Theories on Subsequently Considered Evidence." *Journal of Personality and Social Psychology* 37 (11): 2098–2109.
https://doi.org/10.1037/0022-3514.37.11.2098.

Lunsford, Andrea A. 1979. "Aristotelian vs. Rogerian Argument: A Reassess-
ment." *College Composition and Communication* 30 (2): 146–51. https://doi
.org/10.2307/356318.

Lunsford, Andrea A., John Ruszkiewicz, and Keith Walters. 2016. *Everything's an
Argument.* 7th ed. Boston: Bedford St. Martin's.

Lynch, Dennis A. 1998. "Rhetorics of Proximity: Empathy in Temple Grandin
and Cornell West." *Rhetoric Society Quarterly* 28 (1): 5–23. https://doi.org/10
.1080/02773949809391110.

Lynch, Michael P. 2016. *The Internet of Us: Knowing More and Understanding Less
in the Age of Big Data.* New York: Liveright.

Malik, Kenan. 2016. "All the Fake News That Was Fit to Print." *New York Times,*
December 4. Accessed June 4, 2017. https://www.nytimes.com/2016/12/04
/opinion/all-the-fake-news-that-was-fit-to-print.html.

Manjoo, Farhad. 2017. "Can Facebook Fix Its Own Worst Bug?" *New York Times
Magazine,* April 25. https://www.nytimes.com/2017/04/25/magazine/can
-facebook-fix-its-own-worst-bug.html.

Mar, Raymond A., Keith Oatley, Maja Djikic, and Justin Mullin. 2011. "Emotion
and Narrative Fiction: Interactive Influences Before, During, and After
Reading." *Cognition and Emotion* 25 (5): 818–33. https://doi.org/10.1080/0
2699931.2010.515151.

Marcus, Ruth. 2016. "Welcome to the Post-Truth Presidency." *Washington Post,*
December 2. Accessed June 2, 2017. https://www.washingtonpost.com/op
inions/welcome-to-the-post-truth-presidency/2016/12/02/baaf630a-b8cd
-11e6-b994-f45a208f7a73_story.html?utm_term=.abf7dde52090.

McComiskey, Bruce. 2000. *Teaching Composition as a Social Process.* Logan: Utah
State University Press. https://doi.org/10.2307/j.ctt46nx11.

McComiskey, Bruce. 2017. *Post-Truth Rhetoric and Composition.* Logan: Utah State
University Press. https://doi.org/10.2307/j.ctt1w76tbg.

McEvers, Kelly. 2016. "Stanford Study Finds Most Students Vulnerable to Fake
News." Interview with Sam Wineburg. NPR, November 22. https://www.npr

.org/2016/11/22/503052574/stanford-study-finds-most-students-vulnera
ble-to-fake-news.

McLeod, Susan H. 1997. *Notes on the Heart: Affective Issues in the Writing Classroom.*
Carbondale: Southern Illinois University Press.

Meet the Press. 2017. "Conway: Press Secretary Gave Alternative Facts." NBC News.
https://www.nbcnews.com/meet-the-press/video/conway-press-secretary
-gave-alternative-facts-860142147643.

Melzer, Dan. 2014. *Writing Assignments across the Disciplines.* Logan: Utah State
University Press.

Menand, Louis. 2009. "Show or Tell?" *New Yorker,* June 8. https://www.newyor
ker.com/magazine/2009/06/08/show-or-tell.

Menchen-Trevino, Ericka, and Eszter Hargittai. 2011. "Young Adults' Credibility Assessment of Wikipedia." *Information Communication and Society* 14 (1):
24–51. https://doi.org/10.1080/13691181003695173.

Meyer, Sheree L. 1993. "Refusing to Play the Confidence Game: The Illusion
of Mastery in the Reading/Writing of Texts." *College English* 55 (1): 46–63.
https://doi.org/10.2307/378364.

Micciche, Laura R. 2002. "More Than a Feeling: Disappointment and WPA
Work." *College English* 64 (4): 432–58. https://doi.org/10.2307/3250746.

Micciche, Laura R. 2007. *Doing Emotion: Rhetoric, Writing, Teaching.* Portsmouth,
NH: Boynton/Cook.

Microsoft. n.d. "Microsoft by the Numbers." https://news.microsoft.com/bythe
numbers/planet-office.

Miller, Patricia Roberts. 2016. *How the Teaching of Rhetoric Has Made Trump Possible*
(blog). September 26. Accessed June 12, 2017. http://www.patriciaroberts
miller.com/how-the-teaching-of-rhetoric-has-made-trump-possible/.

Miller, Richard E. 1999. "Critique's the Easy Part: Choice and the Scale of
Relative Oppression." In *Kitchen Cooks, Plate Twirlers, and Troubadours,* ed.
Diana George, 3–13. Portsmouth, NH: Boynton/Cook.

Miller, Richard E. 2016. "Digital Reading." *Pedagogy* 16 (1): 153–64. https://doi.org
/10.1215/15314200-3158717.

Miller, Richard E., and Ann Jurecic. 2015. *Habits of the Creative Mind.* New York:
Bedford St. Martin's.

Miller, Thomas P., and Adele Leon, eds. 2017. *Literacy in Composition Studies* 5
(2) (special issue).

Moffett, James. 1968. *Teaching the Universe of Discourse.* Upper Montclair, NJ:
Boynton/Cook.

Mosely, Milka Mustenikova. 2006. "The Truth about High School English." In
What Is College-Level Writing? ed. Patrick Sullivan and Howard Tinberg, 58–68.
Urbana, IL: National Council of Teachers of English.

Muckelbauer, John. 2008. *The Future of Invention: Rhetoric, Post-Modernism, and the
Problem of Change.* Albany: State University of New York Press.

Mullin, Benjamin. 2016. "How the Washington Post Is Using Genius to Explain
the Twists and Turns of a Crazy Election." *Poynter.org,* July 13. https://www
.poynter.org/2016/2016-annotated-how-the-washington-post-has-used-gen
ius-to-explain-the-twists-and-turns-of-a-crazy-election/421217/.

Murphy, James J. 2012. "Roman Writing Instruction as Described by Quintilian."

In *A Short History of Writing Instruction*, ed. James J. Murphy, 36–76. New York: Routledge.

Mutnick, Deborah. 1998. "Rethinking the Personal Narrative: Life-Writing and Composition Pedagogy." In *Under Construction: Working at the Intersections of Composition Theory, Research, and Practice*, ed. Christine Farris and Chris M. Anson, 79–92. Logan: Utah State University Press. https://doi.org/10.2307/j.ctt46nrqf.9.

National Assessment of Educational Progress. 2016. *Are the Nation's Twelfth-Graders Making Progress in Mathematics and Reading?* https://nationsreport card.gov/reading_math_g12_2013/#/.

National Governors Association Center for Best Practices and Council of Chief State School Officers. 2010. "Common Core State Standards for English Language Arts and Literacy in History/Social Studies, Science, and Technical Subjects." Washington, DC. http://www.corestandards.org/ELA-Literacy/.

Newkirk, Thomas. 2013. "Speaking Back to the Common Core." In *Holding On to Good Ideas in a Time of Bad Ones*, ed. Thomas Newkirk, 1–7. Portsmouth, NH: Heinemann.

Newkirk, Thomas. 2017. *(embarrassment) and the Emotional Underlife of Learning.* Portsmouth, NH: Heinemann.

Nguyen, C. Thi. 2018. "Escape the Echo Chamber." Aeon.co. Accessed April 30, 2018. https://aeon.co/essays/why-its-as-hard-to-escape-an-echo-chamber-as-it-is-to-flee-a-cult.

Nickerson, Raymond S. 1998. "Confirmation Bias: A Ubiquitous Phenomenon in Many Guises." *Review of General Psychology* 2 (2): 175–220. https://doi.org/10.1037/1089-2680.2.2.175.

Nilson, Linda B. 2015. "Getting Students to Do the Reading." National Education Association. http://www.nea.org/home/34689.htm.

Oatley, Keith. 2012. "The Cognitive Science of Fiction." *Wiley Interdisciplinary Reviews: Cognitive Science* 3 (4): 425–30. https://doi.org/10.1002/wcs.1185.

Oatley, Keith, and P. N. Johnson-Laird. 2014. "Cognitive Approaches to Emotions." *Trends in Cognitive Sciences* 18 (3): 134–40. https://doi.org/10.1016/j.tics.2013.12.004.

Obama, Barack. 2006. "Obama to Graduates: Cultivate Empathy." *Northwestern University News*, June 19. http://www.northwestern.edu/newscenter/stories/2006/06/barack.html.

"Performance on SAT Verbal/Critical Reading and Writing Exams." 2016. *Humanities Indicators, American Academy of Arts and Sciences.* www.humanitiesin dicators.org/content/indicatordoc.aspx?i=23.

Perkins, David N., and Gavriel Salomon. 2012. "Knowledge to Go: A Motivational and Dispositional View of Transfer." *Educational Psychologist* 47 (3): 248–58. https://doi.org/10.1080/00461520.2012.693354.

Peterson, Michael Bang. 2016. "Evolutionary Political Psychology." In *The Handbook of Evolutionary Psychology*, vol. 2, ed. David M. Buss, 1084–1106. Hoboken, NJ: Wiley and Sons.

Petrosky, Anthony R. 1982. "From Story to Essay: Reading and Writing." *College Composition and Communication* 33 (1): 19–36.

Pilkington, Ed. 2017. "One Nation, Two Trumps: America as Divided as Ever after First 100 Days." The *Guardian*, April 17. https://www.theguardian.com/us-news /2017/apr/27/donald-trump-first-100-days-president-ohio-voters.

Project SAILS. 2017. *Standardized Assessment of Information Literacy Skills*. https://www .projectsails.org/Home.

Purdy, James P. 2012. "Why First-Year College Students Select Online Research Resources as Their Favorite." *First Monday* 17 (9-3). http://journals.uic.edu /ojs/index.php/fm/article/view/4088/3289. https://doi.org/10.5210/fm .v0i0.4088.

Qualley, Donna. 1997. *Turns of Thought*. New York: Heinemann.

Quandahl, Ellen. 2003. "A Feeling for Aristotle." In *A Way to Move: Rhetorics of Emotion and Composition Studies*, ed. Dale Jacobs and Laura R. Micciche, 11–22. Portsmouth, NH: Boynton/Cook.

Quintilian. 2001. *The Orator's Education, Books 9–10*. Trans. Donald A. Russell. Cambridge, MA: Harvard University Press.

Richman, Matt. 2016. "Millennials Prefer Microsoft Word for Individual Work, Google Docs for Collaborative Work." *Recode*, July 29. https://www.recode .net/2016/7/29/12312086/millenials-microsoft-word-google-docs-collabo ration-study.

Richmond, Kia Jane. 2002. "Repositioning Emotions in Composition Studies." *Composition Studies* 30 (1): 67–82.

Ricks, Thomas E. 2017. *Churchill and Orwell: The Fight for Freedom*. New York: Penguin.

Rosenblatt, Louise. 1983. *Literature as Exploration*, 4th ed. New York: Modern Language Association.

Rosenblatt, Louise. 2005. *Making Meaning with Texts*. Portsmouth, NH: Heinemann.

Ross, Lee, Mark R. Lepper, and Michael Hubbard. 1975. "Perseverance in Self-Perception and Social Perception: Biased Attributional Processes in the Debriefing Paradigm." *Journal of Personality and Social Psychology* (32): 880–92.

Royster, Jacqueline Jones. 2000. *Traces of a Stream: Literacy and Social Change among African American Women*. Pittsburgh: Pittsburgh University Press. https://doi.org/10.2307/j.ctt6wrb9s.

Salvatori, Mariolina. 1996. "Conversations with Texts: Reading in the Teaching of Composition." *College English* 58 (4): 440–54.

Salvatori, Mariolina Rizzi. 2002. "The Scholarship of Teaching: Beyond the Anecdotal." *Pedagogy* 2 (3): 297–310. https://doi.org/10.1215/15314200-2-3 -297.

Scardamalia, Maria, and Carl Brereiter. 1991. "Literate Expertise." In *Toward a General Theory of Expertise: Prospects and Limits*, ed. K. Anders Ericsson and Jacqui Smith, 172–94. Cambridge: Cambridge University Press.

Scholes, Robert. 1986. *Textual Power*. New Haven, CT: Yale University Press.

Scholes, Robert. 2002. "The Transition to College Reading." *Pedagogy* 2 (2): 165–72. https://doi.org/10.1215/15314200-2-2-165.

Seidenberg, Steven. 2017. "Yesterday's (Fake) News." *ABA Journal* (July): 53–55.

Shapiro, Daniel. 2016. "Why We Are Addicted to Divisive Politics." *Time.com*, April 18. http://time.com/4287064/negotiating-the-nonnegotiable/.

Shaugnessey, Mina. 1979. *Errors and Expectations*. Oxford: Oxford University Press.

Shuman, Amy. 2005. *Other People's Stories: Entitlement Claims and the Critique of Empathy*. Urbana: University of Illinois Press.

Singer, Alan. 2014. "Uncommon Core Heightens Race and Class Math Divide." *Huffington Post*, March 10. https://www.huffingtonpost.com/alan-singer/common-core-race-divide_b_4930714.html.

Smagorinsky, Peter. 1992. "How Reading Model Essays Affects Writers." In *Reading/Writing Connections: Learning from Research*, ed. Judith W. Irwin and Mary Anne Doyle, 160–76. Newark, DE: International Reading Association.

Smagorinsky, Peter. 2001. "If Meaning Is Constructed, What Is It Made From? Toward a Cultural Theory of Reading." *Review of Educational Research* 71 (1): 133–69. https://doi.org/10.3102/00346543071001133.

Stanford History Education Group. 2016. *Evaluating Information: The Cornerstone of Civic Online Reasoning*. Stanford, CA, November 22. https://purl.stanford.edu/upload/fv751yt5934.

Storbeck, Justin, and Gerald L. Clore. 2007. "On the Interdependence of Cognition and Emotion." *Cognition and Emotion* 21 (6): 1212–37. https://doi.org/10.1080/02699930701438020. https://www.ncbi.nlm.nih.gov/pmc/articles/PMC2366118/.

Sullivan, Patrick. 2012. "Essential Habits of Mind for College Readiness." *College English* 74 (6): 547–51.

Sullivan, Patrick. 2014. *A New Writing Classroom: Listening, Motivation, and Habits of Mind*. Logan: Utah State University Press. https://doi.org/10.7330/9780874219449.

Sullivan, Patrick, and Howard Tinberg, eds. 2006. *What Is "College-Level" Writing?* Urbana, IL: National Council of Teachers of English.

Sullivan, Patrick, Howard Tinberg, and Sheridan Blau, eds. 2010. *What Is "College-Level" Writing, vol. 2: Assignments, Readings, and Student Writing Samples*. Urbana, IL: National Council of Teachers of English.

Sullivan, Patrick, Howard Tinberg, and Sheridan Blau, eds. 2017. *Deep Reading: Teaching Reading in the Writing Classroom*. Urbana, IL: National Council of Teachers of English.

Sweeny, Kate, Darya Melnyk, Wendi Miller, and James A. Shepperd. 2010. "Information Avoidance: Who, What, When, and Why." *Review of General Psychology* 14 (4): 340–53.

Tannen, Deborah. 1998. *The Argument Culture: Moving from Debate to Dialogue*. New York: Random House.

Teich, Nathaniel. 1987. "Rogerian Problem-Solving and the Rhetoric of Argumentation." *Journal of Advanced Composition* 7 (1–2): 52–61.

Tierney, Robert J., and P. David Pearson. 1983. "Toward a Composing Model of Reading." *Language Arts* 60 (5): 568–80.

Tompkins, Jane. 1996. *A Life in School: What the Teacher Learned*. New York: Basic Books.

Vogel, Elizabeth. 2009. "'Outlaw Emotions' and the Other: Examining the Political Roles and Potential of Emotions in the College Writing Classroom." *Journal of Teaching Writing* 25 (2): 199–222.

Vosoughi, Soroush, Deb Roy, and Sinan Aral. 2018. "The Spread of True and False News Online." *Science* 359 (6380): 1146–51.

White, Brian. 2015. "John Dewey, the Common Core, and the Teaching of English." *English Education* 48 (1): 11–40.

Wimsatt, W. K., Jr., and M. C. Beardsley. 1949. "The Affective Fallacy." *Sewanee Review* 57 (1): 31–55.

Woolf, Virginia. 1957. *A Room of One's Own*. New York: Harvest.

Woolf, Virginia. 2003. "How Should One Read a Book?" In *The Second Common Reader*, ed. Virginia Woolf, 258–70. London: Harcourt.

Wooten, Courtney Adams, Jacob Babb, Kristi Murray Costello, and Kate Navickas. Forthcoming. *The Things We Carry: Strategies for Recognizing and Negotiating Emotional Labor in Writing Program Administration*.

Worsham, Lynn. 1998. "Going Postal: Pedagogical Violence and the Schooling of Emotion." In *Beyond the Corporate University*, ed. Henry A. Giroux and Kostas Myrsiades, 229–65. Oxford: Rowman and Littlefield.

Worthen, Molly. 2017. "The Evangelical Roots of Our Post-Truth Society." *New York Times Sunday Review*, April 13. https://www.nytimes.com/2017/04/13/opin ion/sunday/the-evangelical-roots-of-our-post-truth-society.html.

WPA Outcomes Statement for First-Year Composition. 2014. Council of Writing Program Administrators. http://wpacouncil.org/positions/outcomes.html.

Young, Richard E., Alton L. Becker, and Kenneth L. Pike. 1970. *Rhetoric: Discovery and Change*. New York: Harcourt.

Zimdars, Melissa. 2016. "My 'Fake News List' Went Viral: But Made-up Stories Are Only Part of the Problem." https://www.washingtonpost.com/postevery thing/wp/2016/11/18/my-fake-news-list-went-viral-but-made-up-stories-are -only-part-of-the-problem/?utm_term=.7e935d98d5c1.

Zimmerman, Jess. 2017. "It's Time to Give Up on Facts." *Slate*. http://www.slate.com/ articles/health_and_science/science/2017/02/counter_lies_with_emo tions_not_facts.html.

ACKNOWLEDGMENTS

I would like to express my sincere gratitude to Michael Spooner at Utah State University Press for supporting this book project and for being such an encouraging and generous editor. I am especially grateful that I was able to sneak in one last book under Michael's editorship before he moved on to other endeavors. I would also like to thank Rachael Levay, who saw this book through to its publication. Although Rachael inherited this project from Michael, she has never been less than enthusiastic about it, and for that I am so grateful. I thank the two anonymous reviewers whose comments helped me clarify and refine my ideas, as well as my stance toward the highly charged subject of this book and this deeply fraught moment in our country's history. In addition, I appreciate how carefully Laura Furney, Beth Svinarich, Karli Fish, Cheryl Carnahan, and Daniel Pratt prepared this manuscript for publication.

Finally, I would like to thank my husband, David, and my sons, Avi and Harris, who not only gave me the time and space I needed to complete this particularly time-sensitive project but also put up with the piles of papers and books that took over half of our living room, my preferred working space for the duration of this project.

ABOUT THE AUTHOR

ELLEN C. CARILLO is associate professor of English at the University of Connecticut and the writing program coordinator at its Waterbury Campus. She is the author of *Securing a Place for Reading in Composition: The Importance of Teaching for Transfer* (Utah State University Press, 2015) and *A Writer's Guide to Mindful Reading* (WAC Clearinghouse, 2017). Ellen's scholarship on reading-writing connections and related subjects has appeared in several journals and edited collections. She is co-founder of the Role of Reading in Composition Studies Special Interest Group of the Conference on College Composition and Communication (CCCC) and regularly presents her scholarship at regional and national conferences. Ellen has been awarded grants from the Northeast Modern Language Association (NeMLA), CCCC, and the Council of Writing Program Administrators (CWPA).

INDEX